ERRATA

First photo section, last page headline, *1971 Memorial* should read *1970 Memorial*.
Second photo section: pages 5 and 6 have been transposed.

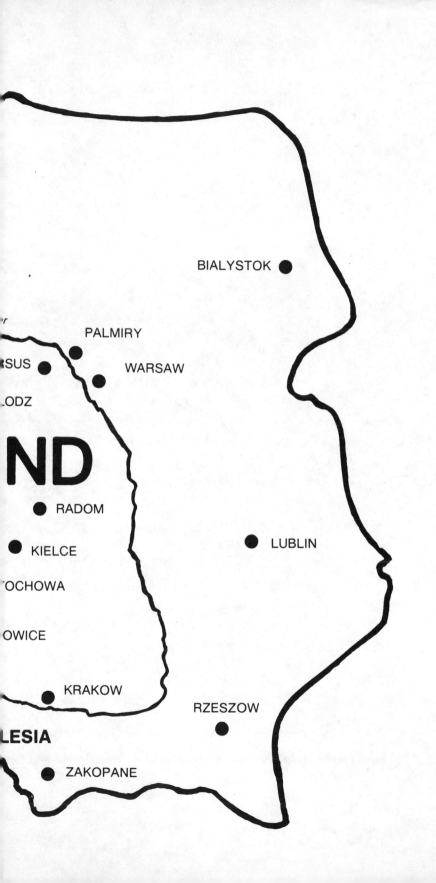

BIALYSTOK ●

r

PALMIRY ●

RSUS ●

WARSAW ●

LODZ

ND

● RADOM

● KIELCE

● LUBLIN

OCHOWA

OWICE

KRAKOW ●

RZESZOW ●

LESIA

ZAKOPANE ●

SOLIDARITY

POLAND IN THE SEASON

OF ITS PASSION

Lawrence Weschler

Foreword by William W. Winpisinger,
International President, International Association of
Machinists and Aerospace Workers

A Fireside Book
Published by Simon and Schuster
New York

portions of this book previously appeared in *Rolling Stone* and in the
November 1981 issues of *The New Yorker* magazine

A Fireside Book
Published by Simon and Schuster
A Division of Gulf & Western Corporation
Simon & Schuster Building
Rockefeller Center
1230 Avenue of the Americas
New York, New York 10020

FIRESIDE and colophon are trademarks of Simon & Schuster.

Designed by Judy Allan (The Designing Woman)

Manufactured in the United States of America

Printed and bound by Haddon Craftsmen.

10 9 8 7 6 5 4 3 2 1

Library of Congress Cataloging in Publication Data
Weschler, Lawrence.
  Solidarity, Poland in the season of its passion.
  "A Fireside book."
  1. Poland—History—1945–   . 2. NSZZ
"Solidarnosc" (Labor organization) 3. Weschler,
Lawrence. I. Title.
DK4430.W47   943.8′05   82-671
ISBN 0-671-44965-6 Pbk.   AACR2

ISBN 0-671-45190-1

For My Mother
with Love and Appreciation

CONTENTS

FOREWORD

At some time most of America's union members have heard or sung or hummed along to a song that's generally considered the unofficial anthem of the American labor movement.

> When the union's inspiration through
>   The workers' blood shall run,
> There can be no power greater
>   Anywhere beneath the sun.

It's an old song. It's been around union halls and picket lines since the early years of this century. It's a legacy of one of the most militant organizations of working people ever known in America, the Industrial Workers of the World. Usually referred to contemptuously as "Wobblies" by employers and the press, the IWW searched out the poorest, most exploited, most desperate of America's working people—needleworkers in the sweatshops of New Jersey, hard-rock ore miners in Colorado, lumber workers in the isolated camps of the great Northwest, hoboes harvesting the grain of the endless prairies.

The Wobblies were the unwashed and the unwanted. A rough, tough, cursing, and fighting group for sure. But they were also a singing group, expressing, as no other organization of working people before or since, the hopes and fears, the optimism and the cynicism, of those who daily go into the mines, mills, factories, and foundries to do America's dirty work. Ironically, the Wobblies are pretty much forgotten today except for their songs. And the song that's lasted the longest and become best known is called "Solidarity Forever." It's sung to the tune of the "Battle Hymn of the Republic."

> They have taken untold millions that
> They never toil to earn.
> Yet without our brain and muscle, not
> A single wheel would turn.

Very few of today's union members know the words. Maybe they've heard it sung at union conventions. Maybe they've joined in a midnight chorus around a hotel lobby after an evening of socializing with their union brothers and sisters in the hotel bar. Maybe they've even marched to it while trying to keep warm on a picket line.

> In our hands is placed a power,
> Greater than their hoarded gold,
> Greater than the might of armies,
> Magnified a thousand fold.

But few of the people who have heard, hummed, sung, or picketed to the stirring strains of "Solidarity Forever" have ever really thought much about the lyrics or what they mean. Workers in America may have been singing of solidarity for a long time. But it has taken the workers of Poland to show what solidarity really means. We know, of course, that the struggle in Poland is by no means over. The workers' movement, which began in the mines and the shipyards, may yet be crushed by the Soviet Army. But in a larger sense the struggle will never be over. While unions can be suppressed and labor movements destroyed, the spirit of worker solidarity can never be fully and finally extinguished.

Moreover, recent events in Poland are not without parallel in the America of an earlier time. Unfortunately, many people, including far too many union members, have forgotten the agonies that had to be suffered in the cause of unionism no more than a generation or two ago.

It was not in Poland but in America, for example, that courts once ruled a union of working people "an illegal conspiracy in restraint of trade." It was not in Poland but in Pullman, Illinois, that a president once sent troops to break a strike. It was not in Lodz but in Ludlow that the women and children of union miners were slaughtered by the hired gunmen of absentee corporate owners. It was not in Cracow but in Chicago that peaceful marchers were massacred by police as recently as Memorial Day, 1937. And it is not in Warsaw but in Washington in this year of 1981 that powerful men have retaliated against the long-building tensions and unbearable frustrations of air-traffic controllers by inflicting massive overkill on that union.

No one yet knows for certain whether the movement known as Solidarity will prevail in Poland or whether such a hopeful manifestation of the human spirit will once again be pulverized by the power of the state. But this we do know: the struggle of Polish workers for democratic unions is but the latest proof, if proof be needed, that the aspirations and needs of working people cannot be permanently repressed even by the most authoritarian system. Similarly, the continuing struggle of American workers proves that even in a free society, unions can never relax their vigilance. In the United States no less than Poland, working people must always stay on guard, remembering that just as Communism naturally breeds its Josef Stalins, capitalism will continue to spawn its J. P. Stevenses.

As long as human societies are divided between the haves and the have nots, between those who employ and those who labor, between those who live off their capital and those who survive by their sweat, working people will intuitively sense the need for solidarity even if they never learn so much as the chorus to American labor's anthem.

> Solidarity forever.
> Solidarity forever.
> Solidarity forever.
> *For the union makes us strong.*

William W. Winpisinger,
International President,
International Association of
Machinists and Aerospace
Workers
November 1981

ACKNOWLEDGMENTS

To begin with, I must acknowledge several nameless Poles—my translator (an absolutely invaluable guide), three taxi drivers, a psychologist, several editors and journalists, several workers. "Oh, don't worry," they used to say. "Use our names. Everything's out in the open. What can they possibly do to us?" Sometimes, indeed, almost giddy with their new-won freedom, they'd insist upon it: "Make sure you use them and spell them correctly. We want to be on record. We want our children to be able to look back and read about this." In most cases—except where individuals were already well known by the authorities or well exposed through their own work—I demurred. In November, when much of this material appeared in *The New Yorker,* my caution may still have seemed excessive. Now, following the desolate events of December, that hesitation appears perhaps more wise. Still, I cannot help but think that even now, even under these conditions, many of my defiant Polish friends would rather have been on record with their names, and I apologize for having less nerve than they.

As for those Poles whom I do mention by name in the pages that follow, I will not make anyone's job easier by listing them here. Suffice it to say that this book came into being through the extraordinary graciousness, generosity, and warm fellow-feeling of many wonderful Poles, and I worry for them.

Carl Ginsburg traveled with me during my first trip, and Henry Feiwel during the second. Many of the impressions and insights recorded here derive from hours and hours of mullings shared with both of them. Conversations with John and Nina Darnton, the Warsaw correspondents for the *New York Times* and National Public Radio, respectively, also proved extremely useful. Anna Maksymiuk, who has in the meantime moved to the United States, was gracious both in guiding me through the shipyard in Gdansk and in helping to sort through some of the intricacies of Polish history once she had resurfaced here. Daniel Singer, one of the most insightful observers of the Polish scene, and his wife, Jeanne, were lovely hosts to me as I returned by way of their Paris home.

Roman Harte, a onetime Polish producer now based at the American Film Institute in Los Angeles, provided me with a series of invaluable initial contacts in Poland. On the other side of the work, Debbie Young and, again, Carl Ginsburg provided splendid assistance in preparing the chronology, and Cheryl Moch proved a tremendously resourceful photo researcher.

My own thinking on the general problems of authority and legitimacy—issues which pervade the second part of this essay—was shaped in large part several years ago during my studies with Sheldon Wolin (then at the University of California at Santa Cruz, now at Princeton, from where he edits the seminal journal *Democracy*). My thinking on the specific problems of political organizing and practice owes a great deal to years of conversations with Cheryl Parisi, Wretha Wiley Hanson, and Michele Prichard.

Rob Tiller did an exceptional job fact-checking the piece as it was being prepared, at breakneck pace, for publication in *The New Yorker*. John Bennet provided calm, smooth, and thoughtful direction in what could have been, and never became, a hectic editing process. Jonathan Schell consistently offered his resonances, and they were consistently evocative. And finally there was William Shawn, whose book this is: without his steady support and continuous encouragement, it would never have crossed beyond the musing stage.

—L.W.

Part One

MAY 1981

Just trying to get in, you can quickly see what drove the Poles crazy. For most Americans, the visa-application process is the first exposure to the maddening pace of the Polish state bureaucracy. By the time you're finished, you can easily end up dealing with three separate offices—one in Washington, one in New York, and one in Chicago—each of which shuttles you back to the two others for further paperwork. And at some point you just end up having to wait. During that time, you may have the opportunity to meditate on the *character* of an entrenched bureaucracy's power: *the tyranny of information.* The clerk knows something you need to know, and he not only won't tell you now, he won't tell you when he will tell you. As the days pass and your anxiety increases, you may also begin to sense the *function* of a bureaucracy: in a society on the verge of shaking itself to pieces, where the socioeconomic pressures of modernity are wreaking havoc on the structures of traditional life, bureaucracy serves *to slow everything down.* To a bureaucrat, what and why don't matter in the least as long as he can slow things down.

Somebody ought to write a novel about this purgatory of waiting, you may find yourself grumbling. And then, of course, you realize that somebody already has—Franz Kafka, the insurance clerk of Prague. In realizing this, you also realize that this bureaucracy is not an exclusively Polish phenomenon and indeed, that it predates the imposition of Communism. For decades—centuries—the Middle Europeans have been refining the theory and practice of purgatorial bureaucratics. Poland is merely one of the world champions. Or anyway, used to be.

Eventually, you may give up on the visa process in America and head straight for Europe, where, for some reason, the tyrannical bureaucracy is less deeply entrenched. Indeed, the closer you get to Poland today the less invincible the bureaucracy's authority seems. In Poland itself, that authority is in substantial disarray. My visa, when it finally materializes early in May, in West Berlin, comes so fast that I don't even have time to buy a ticket before boarding the Berlin-Warsaw night train. I figure I'll buy one on board. At the station, I befriend a Pole I'll call Krzysztof—the top d.j. in Lublin, according to his own account. His backpack is bulging with singles, the treasure hoard he amassed during a week in Hamburg, Cologne, and Düsseldorf. He is twenty-five, and his English is derived principally from song lyrics. Nevertheless, as the train pulls out of the station he is able to regale me with stories and pantomimes of his life and good times as an itinerant disc jockey in the country towns around Lublin. He passed some sort of state exams, but it sounds as if he basically free-lances. Organizations or schools call him and he takes his records: he is very up to date and can discourse at length on Aretha Franklin, the Rolling Stones, John Lennon, disco, and even punk. He tells me about a

Polish punk group he once heard named Deadlock; later they merged with another group and formed Crisis, and he believes they made a record in Paris. Their leader, a punker named Mirek, identifies a lot with reggae music—the way it combines rebellion and religion. Language fails us somewhere in here, but apparently Mirek's music grows out of some sort of mystical identification with Our Lady of Czestochowa, the Black Madonna, whose miraculous protection turned back an invading Swedish army in the seventeenth century.

I ask Krzysztof about Solidarity, and his eyes brighten. He doesn't care much about the politics and the economics; what he keeps returning to is how Solidarity has opened up the borders. This has been his first trip to West Germany. He had no trouble getting a travel visa in Poland, whereas a year ago he wouldn't have even bothered to try.

We cross the border—the grim East German customs official giving way to open-faced and easy Poles. About half an hour later, we hear the conductor scuttling toward us down the corridor. I reach for my wallet and suddenly feel Krzysztof's brusque slap. *"Nie, nie,"* he insists, forcing the wallet back into my pocket. The door slides open, and the conductor asks for our tickets. The other people in the compartment proffer theirs, and Krzysztof proffers his, but when it comes time for me, Krzysztof uncorks a torrent of commiseration, explanation, and elaboration. I have no idea what he is saying. The conductor, a kindly, thick-spectacled old hand, seems by turns bewildered, annoyed, and amused. The two of them go at it as if I weren't even there. At one point, Krzysztof telegraphs to me that he is telling the conductor I was attacked in Berlin and my ticket stolen; then he returns to the fray. Finally, the conductor gives up, retreats into the corridor, closes the door, and moves on. Krzysztof is beaming. "Poland, my country!" he exclaims. "These, my trains! You, my guest!" It's a simple question of hospitality. "Poland," he concludes, "free country!"

I arrive in Warsaw at 6:30 A.M. on May 5th (Krzysztof continues to Lublin) and trundle sleepily over to the Hotel Forum. (From all indications, this first week in May constitutes a relatively calm period in the ongoing Polish crisis. Tempers have cooled considerably since the last frenzy—the police action in Bydgoszcz, in March.) As I wait to check in, I strike up a conversation with an American who is checking out. He is the project manager for a sixty-eight-million-dollar RCA contract to build a color-picture-tube factory here that the Poles will subsequently staff and manage. The project, he tells me, was launched in 1975 and is now almost completed. He'll be back one or two more times. RCA has already been paid off except for the final million or so dollars. He leaves for the airport.

Before I can register, it turns out, I have to exchange my travel vouchers. Poland requires the American visitor to buy in advance fifteen dollars' worth of travel vouchers for each day of his stay—thus, a hundred and fifty dollars' worth for my ten-day visa. As soon as you arrive, you can exchange the vouchers for zlotys at the official rate of thirty-two zlotys to the dollar. You must show a record of that transaction before you check into a hotel. I process my vouchers and register for my room. All of this becomes significant when a few seconds later, in the elevator, the bellboy offers to exchange money at the rate of a hundred and forty zlotys to the dollar. Later in the day, taxi-drivers and various gentlemen milling around the hotel entrance offer a hundred and fifty, a hundred and sixty, and even a hundred and seventy zlotys to the dollar.

There are several ways of trying to describe the economic chaos in Poland today. Perhaps I should begin by noting that thanks to, among other things, the country's dismal balance-of-trade deficit and its resultant huge debt to Western banks, Poland's currency, the zloty, is considered virtually worthless not only abroad but even in its own country. There are many items (lumber, for instance) that for all intents and purposes are unobtainable with zlotys but can be readily procured with foreign dollars. This dismal situation has been officially sanctioned through the institution of PEWEX shops—government-run stores that accept *only* foreign currency. Indeed, the government is so eager for foreign money that some items at PEWEX shops sell for substantially less than their Western retail price. (A large bottle of Drambuie is available for $8.40, a large bottle of J&B whiskey for $6.20, and a pack of Dunhill cigarettes for $.70.) There are even PEWEX apartment houses—government-owned buildings in which rent is payable only in dollars. I pass one of these one day. "The only people who live there," my Polish guide informs me, "are prostitutes and priests."

One result of this morbid situation is the vigorously thriving black market in currency. The people who are willing to offer you five times the official rate for your dollar either accumulate large quantities of dollars and then exchange them at a still higher rate or—more often—use the dollars directly to buy otherwise unavailable goods, either for themselves or for steep resale. These exchange practices render all money transactions in Warsaw a bit dreamlike for Americans. On the one hand, wherever you have to provide proof that your zlotys were obtained at the official rate—when you pay for a hotel room, for example—life can be expensive. A passable double room at the Hotel Forum runs eighty dollars (2,560 zlotys). But nearly everything else can be obtained with unofficial zlotys—"Monopoly money," as it's called by American tourists—and once you've crossed over into the black market you reap a double benefit: you can get five times the official rate for your dollar, and everything you'd want to buy can be had for half its Western price. You start living like royalty. Lavish dinners—pheasant, duck, veal—go for between a hundred and seventy and two hundred and twenty zlotys. You can entertain a couple of friends for a night of dinner and film and be hard pressed to crack five dollars. Meanwhile, outside most hotels there are private citizens, usually old ladies, eager to rent you a private room in their small, two-room apartments for between six hundred and a thousand zlotys a night (under $6.50). They'll even be happy to change the money themselves, right along with the sheets.

The Polish government needs the foreign currency so badly that it generally turns a blind eye to this rampant practice. One day, I ask a Polish friend about all the money changers massed outside the Hotel Forum. Isn't it dangerous? Aren't some of them police agents?

"*Of course* some of them are police," he readily concurs. "But they give good rate, too."

It's not so much the police you have to worry about as the con artists. One morning, I get snookered. In exchange for my dollars, this guy is supposed to hand me a wad of thousand-zloty notes. He counts them out, drops the wad, picks it up, and hands it to me. Once he's long gone, I realize that he's switched wads, and I'm left with a bunch of fifties wrapped in a single thousand note. But still I come out better than if I'd exchanged at the official rate! Which is to say that when you trade at the state bank they're literally robbing you blind—in terms of the real value of their currency.

The Muzak at the Hotel Forum is up-to-the-minute Western rock (music which, for that matter, saturates the entire country). The bar is agog with fancy prostitutes—all of them available for ridiculously small amounts of hard currency—and hordes of Western businessmen dazzled by their sudden good furtune. It can get a little disconcerting, sitting there amidst the prostitutes and the money changers in Warsaw, Poland, to suddenly hear Bob Dylan come wailing over the P.A. system, "When you gonna wake up, strengthen the things that remain?" And it can get downright eerie, sitting there at the fanciest restaurant in town, wolfing down your succulent duck, to look out over the plaza at the lines queuing outside a grocery store where a few patchy lettuce heads adorn the window. It can stop your fork dead in its tracks halfway to your mouth: What in the hell is going on in this country?

Which brings us back to my acquaintance from RCA. "What on earth does Poland want with a color-picture-tube factory?" a Western economist visiting Warsaw asks me in exasperation a few days later. "Hardly anyone in Poland can afford a color TV set, and no one anywhere else in the world is going to want a color set made in Poland. The Poles have managed to pour sixty-eight million dollars into a plant that will probably have to be written off as a total loss. RCA is home free with its sixty-eight million, and Poland is left owing that, plus interest, to a consortium of Western banks. Add a few dozen boondoggles like that together, and you end up with a total foreign debt of more than twenty-five billion dollars. And it's not even as though RCA came to them with some hard sell—*they* went to RCA! Back in the early seventies, Edvard Gierek"— Gierek was the head of the Polish Communist Party between 1970 and 1980—"and his boys decided Poland could have a grand economy with color TVs and cars and all sorts of luxury goods. Only, they forgot to build the infrastructure. And they were so scared of outside criticism that they refused to listen to anyone but their closest advisers, who were all a bunch of cowering yes-men. During the past fifteen years, Poland may well have suffered the worst central planning of any economy in Eastern Europe. I mean, take Hungary by comparison. The Hungarians, too, enlisted the aid of Western companies when they decided to build a big manufacturing complex—only theirs manufactures electric-light bulbs. Now, everybody in Hungary needs electric-light bulbs, and if there's a small surplus the Hungarians don't have to worry—they're never going to prove threatening enough on the world market to provoke any multinational corporations into seeking the kind of trade sanctions that Poland quickly ran up against on another occasion, a few years back, when it tried to corner the American golf-cart market. That was another fiasco."

The Polish Communist Party, perhaps more than any other Communist Party in Eastern Europe, was imposed on its people. (In Czechoslovakia, for example, there was a Socialist tradition, and even, in the early days of the regime, a Communist electoral victory.) It was imposed as one of many factors in Soviet national-security considerations following the Second World War—considerations that may have made sense from the Soviet point of view but left the Polish Communists with a tremendously difficult task in achieving legitimacy. They failed dismally. Lacking a solid, organic connection with the country's working class—the kind of connection that had been claimed, for example, by the London-based government-in-exile, which coordinated most of Poland's indigenous resistance during the Nazi occupation—the Party leadership in Poland tended to drift into an increasing insularity. When workers became restless, the Polish Communist Party, instead of addressing the fundamental issue of the roots of authority and accountability, repeatedly tried to buy off its discontented workers with higher paper salaries or with subsidies designed to defer increases in food costs—strategies that the national economy could not support and that in the long run led to a serious undermining of the wokers' real standard of living.

Meanwhile, as public-spiritedness declined among Party officials and managers, a pattern of cynical privilege-hoarding degenerated into a system of rampant petty and not so petty corruption. It's easy to see, for example, how anyone whose job involved contact with the West could quickly conjure an extraordinary fortune in zlotys. Poles refer over and over to the case of Maciej Szczepanski, the head of the state television network, who, it is said, managed to obtain a yacht, a private jet, and a villa in Kenya before his recent ouster. Gierek is said to have spotted himself ten villas around the country; the one in which he is currently living, according to a recent exposé, cost twenty-seven million zlotys to build—funds skimmed off the budgets of a variety of highway and mass-housing projects. Such corruption, in all fairness, is relatively small-time compared with some of the scandalous examples one finds in the West; but in a country as poor as Poland, and one that at least claims to aspire to an egalitarian ideal, this pattern of inequality has been a cause of increasing public frustration. It isn't even the grossest national examples that so gall most Poles; rather, it's the small corruption pervading the country at the local level: the Party boss who can always count on fresh, lean ham; the plant manager with two extra rooms and a color TV in his house.

Whatever the progress of the current political renewal, the economic situation of Poland has been getting steadily—and now precipitately—worse. This deterioration stems in part from the economic effects of all the recent political turbulence—loss in productivity because of strikes, the shorter work week conceded to many workers by the government, and so on; but it is more generally a result of the cumulative damage to the economy of the thirty-five years of mismanagement that spawned the political turbulence in the first place, especially the mismanagement of the last ten years. Giving Gierek the benefit of the doubt, for a moment, one can perhaps argue that his economic master plan made a certain amount of sense in 1970. Gierek hoped to turn Poland into a major manufacturing power. Western banks were only too happy to lend Poland the money to build the new factories, highways, and other support systems, and Western contractors were likewise delighted to oblige. Poland began to starve its agricultural sector in favor of these new initiatives. Gierek and his men felt that eventually the hard-currency profits from the manufacturing would more than make up for the predicted shortfall in agricultural production. Poland would be able to import food and still make a net profit. At first, things seemed to go well, as was to be expected: billions of crisp, hard dollars were giving the Polish economy a good, stiff rush. But several problems began to develop early on, not the least of which was the worldwide recession of the mid- and late seventies. After the petroleum crisis of 1973, the West could no longer be counted on to provide Poland with a market for its new manufactured goods; the country was left with a horrendous national debt, and no way of paying it off. Indeed, by 1981 something like two-thirds of whatever hard currency Poland was managing to muster was going merely to service the *interest* on the debt.[1] The remainder of the hard currency was desperately needed to import food, consumer goods, spare parts, and raw materials—and there simply wasn't enough. The shelves in stores began to empty, factories fell idle for lack of raw materials or spare parts, buses broke down and couldn't be repaired, electrical blackouts and coal shortages became rampant, and productivity in general plummeted. This was the backdrop for the strikes of 1980: Solidarity didn't cause this situation—if anything, Solidarity was caused by it.

Retracting the benefit of the doubt, one should note that there were many economists back in 1970 who predicted that Gierek's initiatives would come to precisely this end. That Gierek and his advisers didn't listen was partly a function of the insular situation of the Party. But it was also the result of a pattern of vested interests: there was a class of high- and middle-level bureaucrats and professionals—Poland's Red bourgeoisie—who stood to reap substantial improvements in their standard of living under the Gierek policy, and they did. While the rest of the country's economy was becoming riddled, many people were making a killing during much of the seventies. (This social milieu has perhaps been best captured in the films of Krzysztof Zanussi—most recently in *Contract.*)

There are other, somewhat related reasons for Poland's current economic predicament. One is the matter of prices. A Warsaw friend of mine puts the matter succinctly: "Prices bear no relationship whatsoever to actual values in this country." Because the ruling authorities—not the market—set prices for most goods in Poland, and because those authorities lack any legitimacy whatever in the eyes of most Poles, when economic factors have dictated the need for an increase in prices the government has seldom been able to make the increase stick. Workers go on strike and extract either compensatory wage increases or price rollbacks, or, often, both—and the government gives in because not to do so would be to raise the question of its own legitimacy. Meanwhile, to cover its flank (so that at least on paper the columns jibe), the government prints up new zlotys. The result is that, since production is based on real factors (supply of raw materials, spare parts, the length of the work week, etc.), the output of products declines while the number of zlotys in circulation increases. More zlotys chase fewer goods. Is it any wonder that the zloty has become virtually worthless in its own country? The problem in this case is particularly vexing because the workers themselves share a certain complicity.

Another source of trouble is the overcentralized character of planning in Poland. "Poland has long had a serious housing problem, for example," a Solidarity staff member in Warsaw explained to me one afternoon. "So the government decided that the way to attack this problem was with huge standardized-housing complexes. They nationalized all the small local construction concerns and consolidated them into these huge operations that could produce only massive gray housing complexes. The trouble was that once everything became so centralized the slightest crimp in supply or deployment tended to bring everything to a stop. If, say, because of our trade deficit we were momentarily unable to afford to import some ingredient for cement, virtually all housing construction had to come to a halt. Meanwhile, the kind of small scale local operations that in the past could have worked around such momentary shortages had ceased to exist. Here's a case where we once had an infrastructure and it's been destroyed."

People who grew up in Europe before the Second World War recall a time when France and Poland were considered the twin breadbaskets of Europe. This year, however, Poland is expected to spend two and a half billion dollars of its scarce hard-currency reserves on food imports. When you ask Poles what happened, the reply you most often get is, "That's a good question. We can't believe it ourselves." There are long-term causes and more immediate causes. One fundamental problem is that, unlike any other Eastern European country, Poland never succeeded in collectivizing the bulk of its agriculture; even at the outset of Communist rule, the Party's hold on the allegiance of the people, especially in the heavily Catholic countryside, was simply too tenuous. The result is that today approximately seventy-five per cent of the country's arable land is farmed by more than three million independent small farmers, who in turn account for seventy-five per cent of the country's agricultural output. This would be fine except that, for ideological reasons, the government lavishes tractors, fertilizers, and other supplies and equipment on its collectivized farms, making it terribly difficult for private farmers to gain access to similar supplies and thereby reducing most Polish agricultural activity to an astonishing primitiveness.

Most of the peasants one sees in the countryside are either trailing scrawny horses or pushing plows themselves. One man tells me he must wait for up to three weeks to rent a grass cutter or a harvester from the government. "By then, the harvest is over," he says. The government charges him three hundred zlotys an hour for the cutter, two thousand for the harvester; in turn, it pays him four hundred zlotys for a hundred kilos of potatoes and eight thousand for a large fattened pig. But, the peasant tells me, most of the tractors have now broken down, there are almost no spare parts, and the collectivized farms are hoarding what few vehicles remain. According to a recent article in *The New York Times,* Polish independent farmers in 1980 received only half of the fertilizer and forty per cent of the fodder they needed to run their farms. In Poland, as in America, young people are tending to leave the country for city life. "Farmers have less money than workers," I was told by a young man working in a field about forty miles outside Warsaw. "The workers spend theirs—whatever little they have left—on pleasure. Peasants never have time or money for pleasure." In America, the departing youths are being replaced either by machines or by a tenant-farmer class. No such compensations exist in Poland.

The government's pricing policy—or, rather, its inability to enforce a realistic one—accounts for further problems. Because workers reject price increases, the government cannot offer farmers prices that would make it worth their while to produce more goods. ("This is hard work," I heard an exhausted peasant tell an anxious city dweller outside Lodz. "If you're so eager for more food, come out here and grow it yourself.") The situation can result in outlandish aberrations. Sometimes the government actually has to sell certain goods for less than it paid for them, and I heard of a farmer who sold the government a given quantity of potatoes, went to the city and bought them back, and then sold them to the government once again, netting himself a tidy profit. More generally, such aberrations take the form of the rapidly growing black market. Indeed, many farmers living close to the cities could hardly be described as suffering: in Gdansk, for example, I often saw peasants driving up to the open-air market in Mercedes-Benz automobiles, their trunks filled with fresh eggs they were selling at many times the official price.

In 1970, Poland was still a net agricultural exporter. But here again Gierek's administration was responsible for a series of almost insane miscalculations. Notably, Gierek's people took it into their heads that meat consumption somehow betokened modernity, so, to the extent that they aided their agricultural sector at all, they focussed on building up livestock herds—at a cost of millions of dollars in Western feed and of billions of zlotys' worth of indigenous supplies—all for a program that never really coalesced anyway.

The practice of small farming in Poland is terribly inefficient even in ways unrelated to the complications created by government policy. At least five per cent of Poland's arable land lies perpetually fallow, in the form of unfarmed boundary strips between the countless small private plots. At some point, a compromise must be achieved; in the meantime, the Polish breadbasket will continue to provide mere crumbs compared to its potential.

The rest of Poland's economy is likewise surprisingly mixed. There is a large sector that is officially state-owned, a small sector that is officially private, and a remarkably large sector occupying an undefined region between the two. Thus, some people own their own homes, some rent theirs from the government, some buy into government-built complexes, some rent out space in the homes that they own or rent. Some can pass their property on to heirs, and some can't. All this activity is subject to the incredibly complicated bureaucracy. The waiting list to get one's own apartment in a government-built complex is currently over ten years long. (A phone, I am told, can take twenty years: one day you simply receive a note saying that your phone is ready; from that point you have seven days to amass the ten thousand zloty down payment, or else you fall back to the end of the line.) In the meantime, Poles have contrived some ingenious ways of burrowing between the cracks of the pervasive bureaucracy—in some cases, almost literally. I met one man who had given up on his waiting list. He and a group of his friends found a Stalinist-style apartment building on the edge of Warsaw, vintage nineteen-fifties. The building had a large, pompously imposing entrance hall, which the friends commandeered, and into which they slotted four apartments and a store. They procured all the supplies and did all the construction themselves. This man currently lives in one of the nicest apartments I've seen in the Warsaw area, and he pays not one zloty for it: after years of trying to fit his particular situation into one of its categories—to figure out how much to charge him—the bureaucracy has either given up or lost track of him altogether.

In recent months, all sectors of the Polish economy have been experiencing extreme constrictions, and the possibilities for ingenuity are wearing thin. The results, everywhere, are the shortages and the lines. "It used to be," my friend in the free apartment tells me, "that when I saw a line, I passed it by—who needed the bother? You could always find your product later in the day somewhere else, without a line. Now whenever I see a line I immediately join it—I'm excited to find a store with anything to sell."

One evening, I attend a Polish film that was shot about four years ago. At one point in the film, the action moves to a grocery store where there are no lines and the shelves are amply stocked with all kinds of goods—the way things apparently were about four years ago. The scene has the audience rolling in the aisles.

"Products appear and disappear, reappear and then disappear again," a woman tells me. "And then sometimes they just disappear for good. It used to be that our stores were stocked with many different kinds of cheese. I haven't seen cheese in six months." The shortages seem to roll from one product to another. During the weeks I am there, there are sequential shortages of milk, sausage, matches, beer, toilet paper, chocolate, and cigarettes. These shortages translate into long lines wherever the items happen to surface. Conversation within the lines often takes the form of intricate analyses of the causes of the particular shortage of the day. With cigarettes, for example, the theory is that enough tobacco and paper exist but that because of the national debt the government hasn't been able to import the specific type of adhesive needed to seal the rolled papers. With matches, some people feel that it's a question of sulfur, others, of wood. The people pass the time of day patiently waiting, parsing all the possibilities, joking over their misfortune. Meanwhile, the country's productivity is drip-dribbling away: everyone comes in late for work.

One of the most fascinating features of the lines is the institution of self-policing. For example, a rumor spreads that a particular store will be receiving a shipment of sewing machines. A line spontaneously forms. The person at the head of the line takes out a sheet of paper and people sign up in order of appearance. After a while, when it becomes clear that the sewing machines aren't coming that day, they disperse. Each morning, they queue up once again to reassert their position in the line—each name on the sheet is followed by a series of checks—and when the sewing machines eventually materialize they are apportioned according to the list. You find the lines everywhere—even in front of police offices, where the people queuing for travel visas or other bureaucratic appointments first register with the woman at the head of the line, with her tattered list.

"These lines," a woman says to me with a sigh. "This is what kills our time. This is what wears us down—the time we waste in strategizing our daily lives. How you have to remember to buy bread on Thursday, because the line's too long on Friday, and that it has to be brown bread, because white won't last till Monday—all these tiny, petty details, cluttering up your mind until you don't have room for anything else." Another acquaintance tells me she feels that the shortages are a calculated strategy on the part of the government to wear the people down, to slowly rob them of hope and enthusiasm. But a third person—a sociologist—feels that while the lines started out as an inconvenience, they are fast becoming an institution. "It's not that bad," he assures me. "This is where people meet, slow down, talk, exchange ideas on what is happening in the country. And then, the miserable situation of our economy changes the dimensions of living—now we take tremendous satisfaction in the smallest things. Just finding two bottles of milk becomes an adventure. A pack of cigarettes can make my day—it feels like a triumph."

Along a low plateau above the west bank of the Vistula in the north-central part of Warsaw stretches Stare Miasto, the Old Town: a quaint cobblestone quarter virtually unchanged since the seventeenth century—except that not a wall there is more than thirty-five years old. Toward the end of the Second World War, after the Nazis had extinguished successive uprisings in the ghetto and the rest of the town, and before the advancing Soviet Army got around to liberating the few ravaged Warsovites who had survived, the Germans systematically levelled the entire city of Warsaw. In the Historical Museum, off the Old Market Square, you can see old films of the devastation: German soldiers spraying emptied buildings with flame and then dynamiting the burned-out shells. But after 1945 the returning residents of Warsaw refused to accept history's verdict. In an extraordinary community effort, they set about rebuilding the Old Town exactly as it had been. Long-lost crafts of metalworking and glassmaking had to be reinvented, masonry and woodwork meticulously grafted. The result, after decades of painstaking work, is a virtually exact replica of the original Old Town.

Nothing happening in Poland today makes sense without reference to its tortured history, and particularly the grim legacy of the war. This is true in two respects. First, however much mismanagement and corruption may have aggravated Poland's current economic situation, Poland is a poor country. Only thirty-five years ago, it lay in total ruin, its housing and its industry completely devastated. Unlike Western Europe, which could rebuild with the aid of enormous infusions of capital from the United States—the one world power whose industrial base had received no damage whatever—the Poles had to pull themselves up by their own bootstraps. The Soviet Union did extend some assistance, but it was in the process of repairing its own overwhelming devastation. It's easy for Westerners and Americans to ridicule the state of the Polish economy, but we must remember that the existence of any Polish economy at all is evidence of a certain dogged triumph. Second, the tragedy of what the Second World War did to Poland highlights the larger tragedy of Poland's entire history. "This low, flat country is the cesspool of Eurasia," a Warsaw intellectual tells me. "Whenever history backs up to either side of us, the chaos and the carnage spill over into Poland." The Polish people may win the prize for history's least enviable geographical placement. During the past five hundred years, their very existence as a nation has been a sporadic achievement: their statehood disappears, reappears with new boundaries, disappears again. Poland exists within the German sphere of influence during one generation and within the Russian the next. ("The thing you must never forget about Poland," a friend in Warsaw tells me, "is that we lost the Second World War.") Amid it all, the Polish people breed martyrs in endless profusion—a profusion reflected, in turn, in the abundance of flowers with which they then adorn the martyrs' monuments. Every few blocks on almost any Warsaw street, you will come upon a plaque commemorating some gruesome carnage, and the plaque will invariably be draped in bright fresh blossoms. Out of this sorry history, the Poles have distilled a fierce, romantic nationalism, and nothing in Poland today makes sense unless you understand that temper.

And no one has understood it better than the Catholic Church. Diagonally across the street from the University of Warsaw, you will find the Church of the Holy Cross. It's a modest baroque structure. Inside, plaques along the side walls commemorate a cavalcade of Polish national heroes: musicians, artists, scientists, political leaders. In one alcove, there's a bust of Chopin. Beneath the bust lies an urn; inside the urn lies the composer's actual heart. The alcove is strewn with flowers, and tiny student badges from Poznan, Lodz, Lublin, Bydgoszcz, Krakow . . . Similarly, in the crypt beneath the venerable Wawel Cathedral, in Krakow, one comes upon the sarcophagi of Adam Mickiewicz and Juliusz Slowacki, the two greatest poets of Polish nineteenth-century Romanticism. In Czestochowa, about seventy miles northwest of Krakow, a miraculous painting of the Black Madonna, Queen and Protector of the Poles—the holiest shrine of Polish Catholicism—draws thousands of pilgrims to the six-hundred-year-old Jasna Gora monastery *every day,* and hundreds of thousands each August, during the Feast of the Assumption. Dozens of priests hear confessions at all hours, while hundreds of visitors—of all ages, in all sorts of garb—jam forward for a view of the shrine's icon, their faces streaming with tears. (For a moment, one fancies oneself not in Central Europe but rather—where? Iran?) Atop the chapel tower, a huge sign announces, simply, "600," anticipating the six-hundredth anniversary, in 1982, of the founding of the monastery, and Pope John Paul II's promised return visit. "Look at that," my Polish guide tells me. "Six hundred years. Compared to that, what can *they* offer us, with their pathetic thirty-six?"

In the battle between Catholicism and Communism for the hearts of the Polish people, only the former has been able to tap into and express Polish nationalism, while the latter's inability to do so accounts in part for its inability to rule. For Poles, the Catholic Church is an organic national institution, the Communist Party an imposed colonial one. In a courtyard at the University of Warsaw, a twenty-one-year-old literature student tells me that she and eighty per cent of the young people of Poland regularly attend church on Sundays—"some as believers, some as some sort of believers." When you try to get a take on the precise character of Polish Catholic belief, however, things become a bit hazy (just as they do when you try to pin a Solidarity leader down on what, precisely, he sees as the future of economic organization in his country). The student tells me that she and most of her classmates tend to ignore the Church's teachings on birth control and abortion. (Polish families are generally modest in size; finding families with more than three children is unusual, at least in the cities.) She also thinks that the Church's posterboard campaign on behalf of Creationism, as opposed to evolutionary theory, is only marginally effective. "For us," she concludes, "the Church signifies patriotism, tradition, continuity, and stability."

One frequently comes upon young men in priests'

robes—you see priests of all ages, for that matter, but the young priests stand out. "They become priests," a friend tells me, "partly out of a religious vocation, perhaps more out of a patriotic one, but also because the priesthood is the path to the finest education—in every field of endeavor—available in this country. The Church preserves and transmits the knowledge of Poland much more than any secular institution."

A highly educated sociologist tells me that although he himself seldom attends church anymore, he sends his six-year-old son to Sunday school. "The Church has preserved Polish history and culture," he explains. "If my son did not receive exposure to the Church, there isn't a single Polish poem he'd ever understand."

But the Church in Poland offers its congregations something even more profound than cultural heritage; fundamentally, the Church extends to the Poles a limitless *solace,* and Polish history being what it is, such solace just about has to be limitless. This became clear to me on the evening, during the second week of May, when we received word that the Pope had been shot. I had intended to visit a regional meeting of the Warsaw Solidarity branch, but the meeting was summarily cancelled. Instead, I wandered into a neighboring church. In the crepuscular stillness, hundreds of Poles were kneeling in the pews; a priest was saying Mass; the organ occasionally underscored the moment's solemnity. Behind the priest, a huge, ornate gold-leaf altar framed a dark baroque painting of the Crucifixion. Here were these people facing yet further calamities: the life of their Pope (doubly theirs) in peril; their own Cardinal Wyszynski old and badly ailing; their economy in shambles; the Russian tanks at the border—in short, a nation, as ever, on the rack. And here before them, as ever, was the dark, strangely calm image of a man splayed in crucifixion, both a figure for their situation and the promise of a kind of redemption, or at least a solace. "Poland," wrote Juliusz Slowacki, the great Romantic poet, "is the Jesus Christ of nations."

Perhaps the most poignant war memorial in Poland lies about ten miles to the north of Warsaw, at Palmiry, in a flat clearing surrounded by birch forest. This is one of the places where, in the early days of the Occupation, the Nazis brought prominent Polish citizens in the middle of the night and herded them together for summary execution. In the clearing today, you find row upon row of uniform cross-shaped headstones—five thousand of them. At the entry gate, an engraved inscription preserves a bit of anonymous graffiti found in a Gestapo prison cell after the war:

> It is easy to talk about Poland,
> Harder to work for Poland,
> Harder still to die for Poland,
> Hardest of all to suffer for Poland.

On the far side of the clearing, rising serenely out of the birch forest, tall and lean and gleaming white, are three simple crosses, the middle one slightly taller than the others. They suggest nothing so much as a benign eternal vigilance.

"If it hadn't been for the election of John Paul II," a young student tells me in the courtyard at Warsaw University, "August, 1980, would never have been possible. I do not consider myself a believer, but even I was choked with emotion at the news. It gave us a tremendous surge of pride—a sense that we were perhaps something after all, that maybe we didn't have to be resigned to all this."

Another friend—a Catholic intellectual now active in Solidarity—tells me, "It wasn't so much his election as Pope as his visit here that June—in 1979—that really inspired the country. Here we were, facing a tremendously complicated series of logistical tasks—setting the itinerary for his trip, making arrangements for several

huge rallies, providing for crowd control, and so forth—
and the government was pointedly declining to help us.
Generally speaking, the authorities were trying to ignore the Pope's visit as much as possible—television
coverage, for instance, was limited. The police pulled
back, made themselves scarce—partly out of tact, I suppose. And so, completely independent of anything that
John Paul had to say, we discovered an extraordinary
and quite unsuspected competence *within ourselves:* we
could do all kinds of things by ourselves, we didn't need
the authorities. We developed communications networks, planning procedures—all kinds of skills that
would become tremendously useful a year later."

The Pope's Masses during the visit drew millions of
rapt Poles, and one phrase of his in particular has fixed
itself in the people's imagination. It was uttered at the
conclusion of a prayer, and has since been inscribed as a
commemorative frieze on the wall outside the shipyard
in Gdansk: "Let the Holy Spirit come into this country
and this ground. Amen." The woman who translated
the frieze for me in Gdansk sighed emotionally and
whispered, "Imagine! He said that in 1979 and then we
had August in 1980. It was as if he said, 'Let there be
light,' *and there was.*"

The relationship between the Catholic Church and
the Solidarity movement is particularly curious. For
while the Church seems to be inspiring all sorts of de-
mocratizing tendencies within society—by way of its
rhetoric concerning "individual human dignity"—it is
at the same time one of the most rigidly hierarchical
institutions around; indeed, it's the only thing in Poland remotely as hierarchical as the Communist Party.
And while the Church has long provided a context for
resistance, the Church during the recent crises has in
practice been a force for moderation—and, some Poles
go so far as to say, for capitulation. There can be no
question, however, that John Paul II himself presides
over the entire Polish renewal like a guardian angel.

Poles will tell you over and over again that John Paul has informed the Soviet leaders in no uncertain terms that if they and their allies should decide to invade Poland he would immediately fly to Warsaw. (The Poles think that this threat is a major reason for Russia's reluctance to invade.)

"The Pope!" scoffed Josef Stalin in 1935, dismissing a request that he sanction Catholicism in Russia. "How many divisions has he got?" The fact of the matter is, as Stalin's Kremlin successors have come to realize, that in Poland today the Pope's divisions are legion.

There is a dark side to Poland's overwhelmingly Catholic consensus. Perfectly thoughtful and sensitive Polish intellectuals will tell you, without a moment's circumspection, that Poland today is probably the most ethnically homogeneous nation in Europe. "Ninety-eight per cent pure" is a phrase I often heard uttered without a trace of irony.

In September, 1939, more than thirty per cent of the population of Warsaw was Jewish, and the proportion was similar in other Polish towns. (More than three million Jews lived in the entire country.) Long before the arrival of the Nazis, the Jews of Poland had been subject to considerable indigenous persecution, and there is substantial historical evidence to indicate that some elements of Polish society welcomed Hitler's invasion, at least to the extent that it promised to solve the perennial problem of Jewish contamination. After the war, hundreds of cadaverous Jews returning from the concentration camps were bludgeoned as they arrived in their hometowns. Thousands of others were chased out. In 1968, an official anti-Semitic purge further thinned the Jewish remnant. This month, as I was touring Poland, the figures I heard for the total remaining Jewish population ranged from five thousand to seven thousand. One person in Warsaw estimated that there are two hundred Jews remaining in the city.

"Actually," a writer assured me, "many Jews are prominent in several sectors of Polish society."

"What sectors?" I asked.

"Film."

"What other sectors?"

"No other sectors."

"I was brought up on three dead languages," confides the narrative voice at the outset of Isaac Bashevis Singer's 1978 novel, *Shosha,* "Hebrew, Aramaic, and Yiddish (some consider the last not a language at all). . . . Although my ancestors had settled in Poland some six or seven hundred years before, I knew only a few words of the Polish language. We lived in Warsaw on Krochmalna Street."

During the early part of my stay in Warsaw, I, too, lived on Krochmalna Street, in the heart of what had been forty years ago a walled-in Jewish ghetto. I read Singer and walked along his streets—Mila, Nowolipie, Chlodna, Leszno . . . The Jews were all gone, the language was gone—not even the buildings remained. Although the Warsovites meticulously resurrected the Old Town, that project of exact reconstruction stopped at the edge of the ghetto. Its streets are now lined by flank after flank of tall gray mass-produced mass housing. Small Polish children play friskily at intersections where Jewish resistance fighters perished in the final days of the ghetto uprising in the spring of 1943. I saw no memorial plaques on the buildings. In a park, I sat reading Singer and wondered in what sense one could even construe this to be the place he had been writing about. Virtually nothing of the Jews remains; all that persists—strangely unaltered by their disappearance—is the surrounding anti-Semitism.

One afternoon, I wander into a park among the housing units where I do discover a large granite-and-bronze memorial to the ghetto fighters. But it is the only memorial I will see during my entire stay in Poland that isn't wreathed with commemorative flowers.

Another afternoon, I wander over to the western rim of what was once the ghetto, through a walled enclosure and into another time. There, in the dense underbrush of a lush forest, I happen upon the Jewish cemetery. Four hundred years of memorial slabs pitch into one another—wedged and tilted gravestones, cracked columns, decaying figurines, cratered inscriptions. The cemetery seems to recede for acres and acres, everything dappled in suffused green light. Deep in the forest, a few men are engaged in a Sisyphean labor of reclamation. From a shack over at one side emerges an old man—stooped, it seems, by the weight of a huge metal Star of David hanging from his neck. An elaborately embroidered yarmulke covers his sparse hair. He introduces himself as the caretaker of the cemetery.

I am with an American friend, Carl, who as a child picked up a little Yiddish from his Polish grandfather. With the help of Carl's thin strands of Yiddish, the caretaker leads us on a tour. He shows us *"quartiers"* of bankers, shoemakers, and scholars. He walks us past the tombstones of *"groyse rebes"*—great rabbis—and then past the tombs of S. Ansky and I. L. Peretz, two of the greatest Yiddish writers, and then into the *quartier* of the Socialists and the Bundists. "We leave them here to continue their debates," he says, smiling.

At one point, we emerge from the thick forest into an empty clearing—a narrow scar of a wedge. "Here is what we did," he explains. "Early on, the Nazis ordered us Jews to provide sand for the cement wall they were building to close up the ghetto—and they ordered us to dig it out of the cemetery. So as to desecrate as little of the cemetery as possible, the Jews moved the graves from this area to another section of the forest and then dug here. Here they dug deeper and deeper and deeper, so they wouldn't have to do more damage elsewhere. In the end, there was a huge pit. Later, the Nazis used it for mass burials."

We walk on, past tailors and merchants and resistance heroes. Some of the graves are surprisingly recent. "Her daughter is in America," the caretaker explains at a tombstone dated 1967.

"What is your family name?" he suddenly asks Carl.
"Ginsburg."

"Ginsburg, Ginsburg," he repeats, in perfectly measured cadences. "Let's see, what have I got in Ginsburg?" He then leads us to Ginsburg bankers, rabbis, doctors, merchants. . . .

From the Jewish cemetery, we walk about a mile to Aleje Swierczewskiego 79, where, according to an old guidebook, we can expect to find the Jewish Historical Institute and a museum commemorating the ghetto uprising. What we do find is boarded up. We pound on the door. No answer. It's a Wednesday afternoon, four o'clock. We start to walk away, and the door creaks open. A chubby, toothless old man in a cheap gray coat appears in the doorway and gestures that the museum is closed. He doesn't speak English or Yiddish (I'm pretty sure he's a Catholic Pole), but he speaks zloty, and for a small bribe he lets us in. You can do just about anything in Warsaw for a hundred zlotys.

The interior of the museum is a shambles. Downstairs, sacred Torah scrolls are displayed in a cracked vitrine, drenched in dust; a large menorah has toppled over. Upstairs, it's clear, there was once a substantial exhibition on the history of the ghetto during the Nazi Occupation. Today, tattered, curled photos slide from their moorings, maps lie torn on the floor. Blowups of faces hang upside down—sad, reproachful, resigned faces. In one rickety glass case, a rusty milk can and a few disintegrating metal boxes are displayed. These are the containers for the archives—archives meticulously collected inside the ghetto, perilously maintained, carefully buried for later recovery, then recovered, unpacked, mounted, and now utterly abandoned to this new holocaust of memory. On the top floor, clots of correspondence spill from bursting boxes—letters inquiring after missing relatives, dated 1945 and '46. Ancient photographs lie strewn all over the floor, fading in the glare of the skylight—families lost to life and time. As we leave, I thumb through the guestbook. There have been only two other visitors this year. One of them has scrawled "Shame!"

Everything I am seeing confirms the things I've heard about Poland from Polish Jews now living in Israel, France, and the United States. Over and over, prior to my Polish trip, I encountered sheer hatred of the country and its people, cold fury in reminiscences of the anti-Semitism that, it was claimed, pervaded Polish society in the years before and during the war. "You think it's a coincidence that the Nazis placed Auschwitz, Birkenau, Majdanek, Treblinka, and so many other concentration camps in Poland?" an acquaintance in New York asked me. "The Poles were only too pleased to accept things that even the Germans wouldn't stand for." A woman in Israel compared the behavior of the Hungarian authorities, who occasionally attempted to protect their Jews and, in fact, saved tens of thousands of them in the last stages of the war, with that of the Poles, who, she insisted, showed little such compassion. "Today, Poland's synagogues are used as garages!" she said. "I hear stories about the lines and the shortages and the hard times in Warsaw," a Jewish emigré from Poland now living in Los Angeles told me, "and I wish I could say I feel compassion, but you know what? It couldn't be happening to a more deserving people." "The history of the Jews in Poland would make a dark book," concluded another Polish Jew, currently residing in New York, "but I'm afraid it's now a closed book. To all intents and purposes, there is no Jewish question in Poland today."

His words were now being echoed in Warsaw by an

old, tired man, probably in his seventies, who is a survivor of the Lodz ghetto. "Look," the man was saying. "Human life consists of the passage between two doors. For the Jews of Poland today, only one of them is open."

I was therefore prepared to close the book—to close the door on my impressions of the Polish-Jewish question. Only, for some reason, it wouldn't quite close.

For one thing, I encounter a few, admittedly feeble signs of Polish concern. Late in my trip, I learn that a Catholic intellectual club is volunteering some labor at the Warsaw cemetery, and that a committee of prominent Polish cultural and intellectual figures is forming to lobby for the preservation of Jewish cemeteries and synagogues throughout the country. Furthermore, on some subsequent visits to the Jewish Historical Institute in Warsaw I do encounter a few people working in the archives. It turns out that the Institute's highly esteemed staff did flee Warsaw during the anti-Semitic purges of 1968, but a few people have come along since, and they are trying to bear a minimal witness—as much as can be borne, given the fact that hardly any of them speak or read either Hebrew or Yiddish. There is talk of someday—someday—opening the display gallery once again.

But the biggest reason for my reëvaluation of the Polish-Jewish question comes in the form of a group of young Jews whom I happen upon during my last few days in Warsaw. They aren't even supposed to exist, as far as everyone else is concerned, but there they are, coming together for the holy days, for the Sabbath meal each week, and for mutual support and enlightenment. In most cases, these people—mainly young professionals in their thirties (editors, mathematicians, psychologists, and the like)—themselves learned of their Jewish origins only during the past several years. Since that discovery, they've been spending a great deal of time trying to integrate this sudden, unexpected knowledge.

"Most of us have the same story," one of them, a psychologist, tells me on a walk through the former ghetto. "We are children of middle- or high-level officials in the Communist Party. Our parents were Socialists and Communists in the years before the war and had virtually no sense of their own Jewishness even then. They were Marxist atheists, and when the war came—or, in some cases, even before—they fled to Moscow. The fate of Polish Communists in the Soviet Union during the thirties and forties was often tragic—many were sent into the Gulag. But they were true believers, and the thing you have to realize about these Stalinists is that even in the face of such obvious evidence of tyrannical excess as the imprisonment, exile, and execution of their friends and relatives, and even when they faced execution themselves, they remained true believers. They could offer explanations for the occurrence of such aberrations: Stalin didn't know; such was the nature of revolution; the long-term success of the Soviet experiment required sacrifice. Anyway, after the war the survivors returned to Poland with the Soviet Army and took part in the early stages of Communist rule in Poland. Only, they were Jewish atheists, and we, their children, were never raised as Jews, and often weren't even told we were Jewish. That was something we learned only much later—most of us in 1968, when we were suddenly being attacked in the street as Jews, when the Party turned on its own Jews (our parents), using them as scapegoats and expelling them in large-scale purges. Most of us continued to try to hide our Jewishness—that guilty knowledge—from others, and even from ourselves, but in the last several years some of us have been returning, as you would say, to our Jewish 'roots,' and we've been discovering one another."

I ask him how many Jews exist in Poland today.

"Oh, that figure you generally get—between five and seven thousand—is ridiculous. There are tens of thousands of people like us, and thousands of others who still don't know they're Jewish. For one thing, among those who survived the war here in Poland there was a natural process of selection: in most cases, they don't *look* Jewish."

I ask him if he expects any sort of Jewish renaissance in Poland.

"It's much too early to speculate. Certainly nothing dramatic, at any rate. Most of us have been supportive of and active in the current political renewal, and the fate of any Jewish revival will inevitably be tied to the fate of the entire Polish nation. If things open up for Poland, perhaps they will open up for us, too."

This surprises me. Doesn't he believe, like most of his exiled contemporaries, that the Poles are by nature profoundly anti-Semitic?

"No, it's not as simple as that," he replies. "The history of the Jews in Poland is an incredibly complicated story, but it certainly can't be reduced to the statement that Poles are anti-Semites."

Over and over, I hear the same assertion from this man and his young Jewish friends, and they all give me substantially the same reasons for making it. What follows is, in all fairness, a simplification, but the basic premise is consistent: that the Poles were never anti-Semitic at heart. They have always been highly nationalistic, a proud, suffering people deprived of and longing for their state. In the past, they were faced with a large Jewish population—a population whose very size proves the prior openness of the Polish people, and particularly the Polish nobility, to Jewish immigration. The Jews tended to keep to themselves, in ghettos of their own choosing. It is easy to understand how during the eighteenth and nineteenth centuries the highly nationalistic Poles might have conceived of these self-possessed Jews as aliens in their midst. The foreign occupying authorities—especially the Russians—exploited that anxiety, playing the Jews off against the Poles, as part of their strategy for dominating both. For example, these young Jews insist that such pogroms as occurred in Poland were spillovers from Russia—that there were no indigenous Polish pogroms. ("Now, the Russians—the Russians were always rabidly anti-Semitic!") During the late nineteenth century, according to this view, capitalism, a foreign import, came to Poland by way of the Germans and the native Jews. Many of the most visible and most brutal large-scale enterprises—especially textile plants—were owned by Jews. "Polish resentment was understandable," I am told. Poles who couldn't get back at either the Germans or the Jewish upper class often directed their anger at poorer Jews. "It's not pretty, but it is understandable."

During the twenties, this explanation goes on, the Poles finally achieved their state, but ten per cent of the population was Jewish, and the Jews were still largely concentrated in self-contained communities in urban centers. Many people—both Poles and Jews—felt this presence to be troubling, at once alien and too large. Zionists had their Polish supporters. Other Jews, meanwhile, were active in the Communist Party and were devoted to the Soviet example—this in a country and among a people who had only recently thrown off the Russian imperialist yoke. But although individual Poles were often anti-Semitic, according to this account, there was at no point in Poland's sorry history any state or institutionalized anti-Semitism, as there had been in France, in Russia, in Germany. And the most convincing proof of the relative mildness of Polish anti-Semitism came precisely during the Nazi Occupation: Given that many Poles hated the Jews and most Poles wanted them out, still, these young people insist, during the months between the beginning of the Occupation and the mandatory segregation of all Jews into walled-off ghettos, there were no pogroms in Poland. The Nazis would undoubtedly have allowed them, but the Poles did not indulge such a gruesome license.

"It's admittedly a thin spindle upon which to base a claim to humanism," my psychologist friend tells me. "But there was simply the belief that Poles do not behave in such a fashion. They hated the Jews, they wanted them out, but they wouldn't kill them, because Poles didn't kill innocent, defenseless people. It just wasn't done. And there were many recorded instances of 'anti-Semitic' Poles lodging and hiding Jews through the whole war."

After the war, while most Poles looked to their indigenous nationalist resistance, based in London, geopolitical factors dictated the imposition of the Moscow-based Communist "government in exile," a regime that was disproportionately Jewish. "During the late forties, upward of forty per cent of the Polish Communist Party was Jewish," my psychologist friend insists. Once again, the Poles felt themselves subjected to alien forces.

I ask one of the young Jews if he is offended by the virtual lack of Jewish commemoration at Auschwitz. (Although the situation has improved slightly, until recently the camp was preserved as a monument to "the martyrdom of the Polish nation and of other nations," with the Jews listed, when they were listed, alongside the Hungarians, the French, the Yugoslavs, and other European nationalities.)

"Well," he replies, "that's a typical objection. But one thing that foreign Jews fail to understand is that millions of Poles—of non-Jewish Poles—also perished at Auschwitz. Sometimes when you make that objection to a Pole he'll tell you, 'But the Jews have their own Holocaust memorials in Jerusalem.' And there's a certain validity to that. Furthermore, the reason there were so many concentration camps in Poland was not, as I've heard foreign Jews claim, because the Poles wanted them here, but rather, because as far as the Nazis were concerned, after they finished with the Jews the Poles were slated to be next."

Weren't the 1968 purges an example of Polish state anti-Semitism?

"First of all, you will find few of us who will defend the behavior of the authorities here since 1945 on any question. Second, that campaign was largely internal—not so much a Polish phenomenon as a Communist Party phenomenon. It was actually quite clever. Certain elements in the Party saw a chance to eliminate both the Stalinist fathers and the dissident sons—both the right and the left wings of the Party—and in the process open up several bureaucratic slots for themselves—slots that they retain, by and large, to this day. And, third, it was a pathetic attempt on the part of a manifestly colonial regime to pander to native nationalism, to try to appear more Polish in the eyes of its citizens by identifying and attacking an alien element."

I decide not to pursue the obvious next question: What does it say about a people that their nationalism can be pandered to by way of anti-Semitism?

The young man continues, "But, most important, the true Polish character has shown itself in the more recent period, when various quasi-official groups tried to discredit the current political revival by focussing on its Jewish elements—without any success." He then recounts a joke that is making the rounds: "Question: Why is there such a shortage of soap? Answer: Because the authorities are busy turning the soap back into Jews."

"Don't you find that joke offensive?" I ask, somewhat horrified.

"On the contrary," he answers. "It's a good joke. Anyone who lives here recognizes its subtext—that in the past the authorities tried to blame problems on the Jews, but now there aren't enough left to make the charge credible, so it must have been invalid even then."

What of the fact that Czeslaw Milosz, the Lithuanian-born essayist and poet who writes in Polish, was celebrated as a national hero when he won the Nobel Prize in Literature in 1980, but Isaac Bashevis Singer, who was born in Poland, and whose tales deal principally with life in Poland before the war, was largely ignored in his homeland when he won the same prize two years before? ("A virtually unknown American writer who writes in Yiddish" is how the official Polish news releases characterized Singer. "They've gone and awarded the Nobel Prize to a sewing machine!" was a common joke, I've been told. None of Singer's books is available in Poland, although a few stories have recently been translated and appeared in magazines.)

"Again, it's not as easy as you're implying," my friend insists. "Singer didn't concern himself with the Poles. Read those stories, as I have—I read them in English. Poles hardly ever appear in them, and when they do they are portrayed as shadowy, alien figures. In a fundamental sense, Singer is *not* a Polish writer—certainly not the way Milosz is."

And so forth. It is strange to hear this kind of account from Jews, but increasingly I have come to see these young people not as Polish Jews but, rather, as Jewish Poles—a new breed altogether. These are people who grew up imagining themselves Polish—imbued with the stubborn, fierce, romantic nationalism of their friends and classmates—and have only recently come to their Jewishness and to the difficult task of trying to integrate that Jewishness into their lives.

I don't quite know what I think of their version of Polish-Jewish history. I do know this: Through my meetings with these young Jewish Poles, I have come to a deeper appreciation of the tragic nature of the historical interpenetration of these two peoples in this hopeless land where ironies fold in and in and in on themselves. For, apart from anything else, Polish history and Jewish history seem to illuminate each other. If Poland, as Slowacki claimed, is the Jesus Christ of nations, then we are speaking of Jesus the Jew, the martyr to the Roman occupation of Palestine. The situation of the Poles during much of the last two centuries—a people, a language, a religion, a literature, a culture, all without a state—is uncannily congruent with the simultaneous situation of the Jews. Much has been written of the messianic longing with which Polish-Jewish Chassidism was rife during the early nineteenth century—but Polish Catholic Romanticism during that period likewise conceived of a national messianic mission. It is one of the cruellest ironies of history that these two stateless, visionary peoples came to share the same meagre plot of land at the same moment.

One day, I ask a Polish Catholic if she has ever read the Book of Job—it seems so much the book of Poland.

"Well, it's funny you should mention that," she answers. "As Catholics, we seldom read the Old Testament. But Milosz, in exile in America, taught himself Hebrew so he could translate sections of the Bible, and he's just released an extraordinary Polish version of Job. Many people are talking about it." [2]

Adam Michnik, one of the leading theorists of the current political renewal, and himself a Jew (though not a particularly observant one), recently wrote an article in which he cast 1956, 1968, 1970, and 1976 as "dates which stake out the successive stations on the Polish *via dolorosa.*" There is a poster that summons the same theme through different imagery. A bright-red pulse line moves horizontally across a white background—a seismograph, or perhaps the record of a heartbeat—erupting periodically in steep, jagged verticals, above which are the dates '44, '56, '68, '70, '76, '80.

Approaching the present, the tremors increase in strength and frequency, and on the other side of 1980 the red line opens out onto a single powerful word: "SOLIDARNOSC."

Of all the lines in Warsaw this May, one of the longest always seemed to be queuing outside a small building on the edge of the Old Town. People stood patiently waiting for up to two hours at a time, not for food or supplies or bureaucratic approvals, but to see a spare exhibit, compiled by a local photo club, of photographs and documents from "The Events of the Years 1956, 1968, 1970, 1976, and 1980." The unofficial exhibition (it was never advertised in the regular newspapers) consisted of amateur documentation of events that officially had hardly happened at all.

Once inside the building the line snaked slowly along the perimeters of three small adjoining rooms; at eye level, a cavalcade of photos had been modestly pasted to the walls. The quality of the photos was generally crude, hasty in execution, haphazard in preservation. The originals of the photos had been surfacing over the past several months, often anonymously, at Solidarity offices around the country. They had been taken, often on the run, usually with primitive equipment, by individuals who subsequently risked imprisonment just by keeping them in their homes. In ironic and often outrageous juxtaposition to the photographic record, the organizers of the show sometimes displayed copies of contemporary official accounts of the same incidents. Thus, for example, beside photos of the mass protest rallies in Poznan in 1956 were newspaper articles describing "the machinations of a small band of provocateurs."

In 1956: Stalin had been dead for three years when Nikita Khrushchev launched the process of de-Stalinization with his famous secret speech to the Twentieth Congress of the Soviet Communist Party, in February. That process, unsettling as it was within the Soviet

Union itself, was wrenching along the periphery of the Soviet empire. In June, in the most dramatic of the Polish confrontations during this period, workers from the Zispo engine plant, in Poznan, set down their tools and marched on the town center, angrily protesting food prices and scarcity. Shots were fired; there were some deaths and many injuries. In the fall, Wladyslaw Gomulka, a popular nationalist who was by no means the first choice of the Soviet authorities (indeed, he had spent time in Stalinist prisons) was rehabilitated and installed as Party Secretary, inaugurating the famous "Spring in October," a period of renewal as hopeful as it was short-lived. (The attention of the Soviet authorities had in the meantime been distracted by events in Hungary, whose rebellion began as a series of demonstrations in sympathy with the Poles.)

In 1968: Gomulka's regime had stiffened into a traditional autocratic bureaucracy. (Four years earlier, Jacek Kuron and Karol Modzelewski had been expelled from the Communist Party for suggesting, in an "Open Letter to Communist Party Members," that "state ownership of the means of production" did not necessarily produce "social ownership" of those means—and, indeed, that Communism as it was currently being practiced in Poland had veered profoundly from Marxist first principles.) Discontent was rising, particularly among students and intellectuals. (This was the season of youth movements in Prague, Paris, Berkeley, and Chicago.) By March, the authorities had maneuvered the students into a situation in which they were forced to stage a protest without adequate preparation. The regime responded to this—its own provocation—with a double attack. First, "angry workers" were brought in from the outskirts of various towns, especially Warsaw, to beat up the demonstrating students. (It should be noted that although relatively few workers actually participated in the thuggery, still fewer came to the defense of the students;

the "generation gap" of those years was, after all, a global phenomenon, and in Poland the separation between intellectuals and laborers was still quite severe.) Second, certain elements in the Party, including Gomulka himself, launched their rabid anti-Semitic campaign.

In 1970: By December, the economic consequences of Gomulka's tenure had become so serious that the government was forced to post a series of shocking price increases. In a clumsy ruse, the government tried to disguise the increases as a "rearrangement" of prices— the prices for luxury items like television sets, car radios, and tape recorders were lowered, while the prices for necessities like food and clothing went up. The announcement created unrest throughout the country, culminating, in the middle of the month, in a complete shutdown of the shipyards in the Baltic Coast cities of Gdansk, Gdynia, and Szczecin. The workers poured out of the yards, marching on the town centers. (The intellectuals, nursing their wounds from two years earlier, on the whole declined to join or support the demonstrations.) On December 16th, the government responded with a terrifying display of force, ordering "Polish soldiers to fire on Polish workers"—as the dark incidents were recalled afterward. Helicopters dropped tear gas on the crowds of surging demonstrators; tanks sprayed machine-gun fire. Dozens, perhaps hundreds, were killed; thousands were injured. No one knows the exact figures; the incidents themselves were quickly cloaked in official silence. Nevertheless, the rebellion did have substantive results: Gomulka was ousted, to be replaced by Gierek; and within a few months, after a decisive follow-up strike by the women textile workers of Lodz, the new government rescinded the price increases.

In 1976: The boom of Gierek's early years, financed largely by foreign loans, had gone bust. But when Gierek tried once again to raise food prices in order to shore up his faltering economy, he, too, faced a work-ers' veto. This time, the disturbances were most pro-nounced at the Ursus tractor plant, outside Warsaw, and in Radom, a town about sixty miles south of the capital that was the site of an important armaments factory. The incidents were perhaps not as dramatic as some of the earlier confrontations, but their dénoue-ment proved crucial, for it was in their aftermath that a small group of intellectuals formed KOR–KSS—The Committee for the Defense of the Workers and the Committee of Social Defense. The activities of these groups, which began monitoring various state cam-paigns of harassment against individual activist work-ers, publicizing trials, interceding wherever possible, and generally raising issues for public discussion, proved vital in at least two ways during the years to come. First, KOR at last transcended the separation be-tween intellectuals and workers that had bedeviled the Polish dissident movement, to the detriment of both sides, since 1968 and, for that matter, through most of Polish history. Second, since many of those associated with KOR—including Jan Litynski, Adam Michnik, and Karol Modzelewski—were of Jewish origin, the organi-zation likewise served to transcend the separation be-tween Catholics and Jews, which might otherwise have been played upon by the authorities in the years to come. As it happened, in 1980, when quasi-official groups tried to play the workers off against the "ex-perts," and the Catholics against the Jews, their at-tempts failed dismally. "We remembered," a worker in Warsaw told me. "Those people had been with us and helping us for several years. The government couldn't fool us again as to who our true friends were."

In 1980: The summer of the Moscow Olympics. This time, the occasion was a rise in meat prices: many Poles felt that their meat was being shipped to Moscow for the festivities, a suspicion which only fueled their anger.

The meat-price decree, issued on July 1st, provoked a rolling series of strikes: workers at one factory would lay down their tools, the government would quickly raise wages and rush in fresh supplies of meat, and the workers would return to work; then, when the workers at a factory a few dozen kilometres away heard about these results, they would go on strike, with a similar set of demands. Warsaw, Katowice, Lublin . . . And then, in mid-August, at the Lenin Shipyard, in Gdansk. Some time earlier, in somebody's idea of a brilliant preemptive move, the authorities at the shipyard had fired Anna Walentynowicz, a fifty-one-year-old widow and crane operator who was an activist and a mother figure to the young workers in the crews. (They called her Pani Anya—Mrs. Anya.) That was stupid. You don't fire the crane operator. She's the most visible person around, and the workers know she's competent—after all, they trust their lives to that competence every day. In fury over such firings and the recent price increases, the workers of Gdansk put down their tools on August 14th and refused to be dislodged from the factory, their fortress: they had learned their lesson ten years earlier, witnessing the worst massacre in postwar Polish history, and they were not about to leave the plant or be appeased by a few extra slabs of meat. The next day, the strike began to spread throughout the region. (August 15th is one of the holiest days in the Polish Catholic calendar—the Feast of the Assumption, and a day particularly consecrated to the Black Madonna of Czestochowa. On August 15, 1920, in an action that Poles refer to as "The Miracle on the Vistula," General Jozef Pilsudski, at the head of a Polish nationalist army, held off an invading Soviet Bolshevik force on the outskirts of Warsaw [3]—further increasing the stature of the Black Madonna in the Polish imagination.) The strike continued for seventeen days, and the victorious workers returned to their machines on September 1st—the anniversary, of course, of the 1939 Nazi attack on the Polish garrison at Danzig—then Danzig, today, Gdansk—which set off the Second World War.

This was the history which that photo exhibition in Warsaw was attempting to document, and which its visitors were drinking in in draughts. The images themselves were interesting, sometimes even poignant, but to Western eyes they seemed if anything almost clichéd: over the years we have become inured to photos of street demonstrations, banners, police phalanxes, hippie beatings. We have seen thousands of images of Selma, People's Park, Chicago, Northern Ireland, and so forth, and the power of such imagery has eroded for us. What was truly fascinating at this exhibition, therefore, was not so much the photos as the extreme intensity with which the Poles themselves were examining them. Never in all my years of visiting art and photo exhibitions have I seen images studied with such care and concentration. People would stand transfixed in front of a single image for two, three, or five minutes before moving a few feet over to the next image, upon which they would lavish similar attention. It was as if they'd never seen anything like it—and they hadn't. The entire exhibit seemed to say, "See, look, those weren't unfounded rumors; we told you this happened, here's proof."

Some of the official accounts had blossomed over with spontaneous graffiti: over one article from the party newspaper concerning the 1956 disruptions, someone had scrawled, "Lies! Lies! Enough lies!" Across another official photo of the 1970 Party Central Committee appeared the word "Bandits!" Some of the dour images of individual officials had sprouted updates: "This murderer Kociolek," for example, "is still on the Secretariat of the Warsaw Party Committee."

A newspaper account of the 1976 troubles in Radom described them as "the work of hooligans." In the photo next to the article, a banner stretched above the throng, insisting "GLODNY ROBOTNIK TO NIE CHULIGAN" ("A hungry worker is not a hooligan"). Other posters read "CHLEB" and "WOLNOSC" ("Bread" and "Freedom"). The moral lesson was apparent: Don't believe everything you read.

Far and away the most powerful sequence of images was that depicting the events of December, 1970. The photographs showed how the Gdansk strikers surged out of their factory and marched on the Old Town, where, stonewalled by bureaucrats, they set fire to the Communist Party's regional headquarters. (In one photo the building is ferociously ablaze, while across the street, on the roof of a nearby church, demonstrators are stamping out straying embers.) Then there were photos of the bullet-spraying helicopters, cordons of advancing militia men, tanks lumbering incongruously through the quaint cobblestone alleys of the Old Town. There were images of crowds fleeing and, in their wake, dead crumpled bodies. There was a surging crowd carrying a lifeless body atop a torn-off door frame. This last photo was draped with wilted flowers.

Standing before one of the images, a former resident of Gdansk held a group of Warsovites enthralled with his recollections. "Right over there"—he pointed to an intersection in one photograph—"I saw a policeman sneak up on a comrade and smash his skull in. Immediately the crowd surrounded the lone officer, disarmed him, and literally tore him to pieces. The officer was dead and virtually dismembered by the time reinforcements arrived. I saw that with my own eyes."

A few minutes later, outside the exhibition, I asked the man from Gdansk whether in the years between 1970 and 1980 he had felt free to tell his story. "Hardly ever," he replied. "If we spoke about such things at all, it was only among close friends. Once, it must have been in 1971, I had to travel to Krakow. Leaving the station, the taxi-driver asked me where I was from. When I said Gdansk, he turned off the meter and drove me around town for over an hour asking me for details of what happened. But in Gdansk, the townspeople seldom spoke of the events of 1970, except with our glances; when things began to pick up again last summer, it was clear everybody had been thinking about it all along."

A week after I visited the show, I happened to meet one of its organizers at Solidarity's national headquarters. He showed me some other photos, and then he prepared to play me a tape. Someone off the street had brought in the original cassette a few months ago; this man had happened to be recording events in Gdansk at the very moment the shooting broke out. He'd kept the cassette hidden for years and never played it for anyone until he brought it to the Solidarity office that day.

At first, the impact of the sounds on the tape—the crackle of bullets, the wail of sirens, the chanting of crowds, the scatter of people—was once again dulled for me by my Western familiarity with the aural vocabulary of violence. But as the tape continued—on and on, shooting, sirens, screams, more shooting, and then *more* shooting—the horror began to bleed through. It occurred to me that our Western newscasts always offer us bite-size morsels, little digestible snippets that disguise the true horror of conflict—that is, that it just seems to go on and on and you have no idea when it's going to stop. The man playing the tape for me seemed no less moved, even though, surely, this was the hundredth time he'd heard it. After a while the tape ran out in mid-wail.

As I was getting ready to leave, the man reached into his cluttered desk and pulled out a file. It contained copies of some of the photos in the show, and he asked me to take about a dozen. "We want copies to exist in the West," he explained. "They need to be published everywhere, so that even if something goes wrong here in Poland, they'll never be able to say 1970 didn't happen."

Two things seem to me important about the relationship of most Poles to this history—this rosary chain of intellectuals. When you ask such people, "Why did '1980' happen in 1980, and not in 1976, say, or 1970, or 1968?" the answer you invariably get is "The moment wasn't right until 1980." This formulation is at once Marxist (the various elements of society had not achieved the appropriate configuration and consciousness until 1980) and Catholic (the Moment comes when It comes). In Poland today, these two categories are ineluctably intertwined.

The second, however, concerns just about everyone in Poland, and it has to do with the truly traumatic impact of some of the massacres that make up this litany of dates—to some extent, Poznan in 1956, but especially Gdansk in 1970. In America, by contrast, although we had our share of violence during the sixties (thirty-five people died in Watts in 1965, at least twenty-six in Newark and forty in Detroit in 1967, four at Kent State in 1970), we got over it. "That's history," we tend to say, meaning, "It happens, it's past, all you can do is look to the future." In Poland, when people talk about the massacre in Gdansk and say, "*That's history,*" the veins in their foreheads pulse and conversation stops dead cold. They *cannot* get over it. Poles, especially the residents of Gdansk, talk about 1970 the way Jews talk about Auschwitz: it's almost a transcendent category. This is partly because the memory of the incident was repressed for so long: virtually no official mention was made of it. The story persisted through word of mouth, glance of eyes, and secretly passed photographs. (Over the years, an eerie, silent conspiracy of commemoration spread throughout the country. Whenever people had occasion to write "1970" they wrote it "19 + 0." This practice spread even to government documents reviewing the period.) But there's something more, and everyone in Poland seems to sense it: If these dates constitute the *via dolorosa* of the Polish people, then 1970 was the Crucifixion, and 1980, by implication, the Resurrection and the Life.

In Warsaw this spring, Woody Allen's *Manhattan* is the big American film. *Three Days of the Condor, Hair,* and *A Star Is Born* are also playing. People still talk about *Taxi Driver.* (One student tells me it was her favorite recent film, "because it portrayed a man who had the courage to be a nonconformist"—so much for what gets lost in the translation.) Last year, *Star Wars* played briefly, without that much success (who needed science fiction?), but *One Flew Over the Cuckoo's Nest* is regularly packing them in. A few seasons back, the authorities heavily promoted *Norma Rae,* a film about union organizing in a textile mill in the American South; they were hoping to educate their countrymen to the horrific realities of capitalist exploitation, but, according to some Solidarity spokespeople, the message that most Poles came away with concerned the fundamental importance of trade unions. On television, Poles receive weekly transfusions of "The Streets of San Francisco," "Columbo," and—starting just recently—"Charlie's Angels" and "Starsky and Hutch." ("Oh, we love to see all those American cars," a Warsaw acquaintance tells me. "And I particularly love the way American phones ring.") But, for a change, the most talked-about movie in Warsaw this spring is not American but Polish, and you can't even find it listed in the paper.

Robotnicy '80 (Workers '80) is a documentary about the Gdansk shipyard strike of that year. Although it was grudgingly passed by the censors (the public would not have stood for its outright banning), it has not been allowed to receive regular distribution, and newspaper advertising is forbidden. On any given evening, it's playing somewhere in Warsaw, but to find out where you have to look in the paper for the theatre where "All Seats Are Sold Out." That's the code. Go to that the-

Start with the logo. Designed during the second week of the August 1980 strike by J. and K. Janiszewski, two marginally employed graphic artists living in Gdansk, it comes surging forward, like a crowd. The N holds its rippling banner proudly aloft—the red and white flag of Poland.

Like its logo, Solidarity, the movement, comes barreling out of a history of struggle in a land where the mere mention of a year invariably summons up a store of common impressions. Witness the poster below with its seismograph (or heart chart) recording the dates 1944, 1956, 1968, 1970 and 1976—a legacy of failed national rebellions—and then opening out, in 1980, onto that simple word: Solidarity. Rooted in that history, the Solidarity movement grew at an incredible pace: Within one year, as its first-anniversary poster reminds us, the organization's membership had swelled from a few dozen to "10-MILLION SOLID."

*The insignia at **left** was the symbol of the Polish Home Army, the indigenous resistance movement which fought the Nazis and was subsequently destroyed by the invading Soviet army in 1944. PW stands for "Polska Walczaka"—"Poland is still fighting"—but the insignia also suggests Poland Anchored (the anchor being a longtime token of Polish Catholicism). Solidarity revived the symbol in its August 1981 poster commemorating the thirty-fifth anniversary of the Warsaw Rebellion, during which the Soviet Army stood by while the Nazis killed 200,000 Polish freedom fighters and levelled the city (Fig. 2). See discussion on pages 113–114 and Chronology.*

In June 1956, approximately seventy striking workers in Poznan were killed in clashes with the Polish army and police. At one point, in an image which all Poles remember, a crowd led by a woman clad in white marched on Stalin Square, bearing a Polish flag which had been dipped in the blood of a fallen comrade. (The image is uncannily reminiscent of Delacroix's Liberty Leading the People.) *In June 1981, Solidarity's graphic designers alluded to that incident in their twenty-fifth-anniversary memorial poster, which portrayed a simple red-and-white bloodstained Polish flag.*

Pilsudski Institute of America

UPI

The most traumatic event in the litany of failed Polish rebellions was the massacre of hundreds of striking shipworkers in Gdansk, Gdynia, and Szczecin in December (Grudzien) 1970. Ten years later thousands of Poles jammed a touring exhibition consisting of amateur photographic documentation of those terrible days (Fig. 6). Some photos from that exhibit are reproduced on the next three pages. Although the government tried to expunge the memory of the 1970 events, Poles contrived various subliminal strategies of commemoration. For example, when writing the year 1970, they took to transubstantiating the 7 into a cross (Fig. 5); the otherwise unmarked graves of the dozens of victims of police violence in the Gdansk cemetery began sprouting anchors beneath their crucifixes, an indication of the fact that here lay a shipworker who had died a Polish Catholic martyr (Fig. 8).

5

6

7

8

Perhaps the single most vivid image of the Gdansk 1970 violence in the memories of most Poles derives from a photograph of a surging crowd bearing at its head the corpse of a fallen worker atop a torn-off door. When Andrzej Wajda made his film Man of Iron in 1980, he painstakingly recreated the scene (Fig. 2), and one of the posters for the film alludes to the event: A white shirt, stained blood red, is spread-eagled across a white background—an image suggesting the crucifixion of the Polish flag (Fig. 3).

2

United Artists Classics

3

Further amateur photographs from the touring exhibition documenting the events of December 1970 in Gdansk. A phalanx of heavily shielded militiamen converges on a protesting crowd; tanks loom incongruously amidst the quaint cobblestone streets of Gdansk's Old Town with its tourist center, the Poseidon fountain; a crowd of angry demonstrators watch as the Communist Party headquarters burns out of control (on the roof of the neighboring church, out of camera range, workers stamp out stray embers). For a full discussion of these events, see pages 43–46 and the Chronology.

Sunday, August 22, 1980, in Gdansk. Following an outdoor Mass at the strikebound Lenin Shipyard, priests hear confession of individual workers.

Just outside the shipyard gates (which have become festooned with bouquets, crucifixes, and pictures of the Pope), the citizens of Gdansk reach up for copies of that morning's strike bulletin which the workers have produced in the shipyard's printing plant.

Inside the strikebound yard, negotiations proceed apace, with every word being piped live over the yard's P.A. system to the 16,000 workers outside. On the left, the strike committee, including (in the lower corner, reading) Andrzej Gwiazda, and at the table, center, Lech Walesa. Facing Walesa (on the right, with eyes closed), is the government representative, Mieczyslaw Jagielski; to his right (wearing glasses) is Gdansk party leader Tadeusz Fiszbach.

A series of sequential strikes rolled through Poland for almost six weeks in the summer of 1980 before reaching the Gdansk shipyards; but, once the strike began there on August 14, it took on a decidedly more serious character—perhaps because these workers still lived with their memories of ten years earlier. For the first time Polish workers demanded the right to form a free trade union; and after seventeen days, they won it.

Anna Walentynowicz, the well-loved crane operator whose firing was one of the initial causes of the strike by her fellow 16,000 shipworkers, addresses them during the early days of the August strike.

Jean-Louis Atlan/SYGMA

Alain Keler/SYGMA

August 31, 1980. The negotiations triumphantly concluded, Lech Walesa stands on top of the shipyard gates to address the thousands of citizens of Gdansk who have supported the shipworkers with food, blankets, and their prayers. They, in turn, chant, "Thank you, thank you, thank you."

Jan Hausbrandt

Henry Feiwel

Henry Feiwel

One of the first demands the Gdansk workers made—and the government granted—in August 1980 was the right to build a worthy memorial to their fallen comrades of December 1970. In just three months, the shipworkers themselves designed, constructed, transported (Fig. 2) and erected the monument, which consisted of three giant crucified anchors, 140 feet in the air. Into the monument's base, the shipyard artisans slotted bas-reliefs of themselves striking, spending time in jail, and even building the monument itself (Figures 3 and 4).

atre and you can most likely get yourself a seat for one of the most extraordinary films of recent years.

Before I saw *Robotnicy '80,* I had occasion to speak with one of its co-directors, Andrzej Chodakowski, a tall, gentle, soft-spoken man with an uncanny facial resemblance to Sid Caesar. "In August of last year, as the Gdansk strike began to develop, it took our unit ten days of intensive lobbying at Film Polski, the government film bureau, before we received reluctant permission to take our cameras up north," he told me. "As usual, the intercession of Andrzej Wajda proved crucial." Andrzej Wajda, Poland's foremost director, is a national hero and often wields his considerable authority to help realize progressive projects in the Polish film industry. "Once we got to the shipyards, it took still more time before the workers would let us in. They had the factory completely closed off and were exercising very strict security, trying to prevent the entry of secret-police provocateurs. They were also particularly suspicious of us because in the past photographs had been used, at the conclusion of a strike, to identify strike leaders, who then mysteriously disappeared. This had happened to hundreds of their comrades in the months after 1970. We finally reached an agreement—they could control the footage until after the successful conclusion of the strike, and destroy it if anything went wrong. Once we were let in, filming proved quite difficult. It was a tremendously emotional time, and there were moments when we ourselves were unable to continue—our own eyes became clouded over with tears. Beyond that, we had been able to secure only thirteen thousand metres of film stock, which we had to ration carefully without having any idea how long the strike would go on. During the final days, as tensions at the negotiating sessions mounted, we were particularly anxious, because we were running out of film. But it all came to a happy conclusion, and a few weeks later, at a special midnight screening at the Gdansk Film Festival, we were able to show some of the early rushes. The auditorium was filled with veterans of the strike, and there in the middle of it all was Lech Walesa, flanked on one side by the Archbishop of Gdansk and on the other by the Deputy Minister of Culture. It was incredible—six weeks earlier, this man had been an unemployed electrician."

In *Robotnicy '80*, the camera is scrunched right in there during the most sensitive negotiations between the strike leaders and government representatives—but then so was just about everyone else in the yard. The government had asked for secret negotiations, but Walesa and his colleagues insisted that everything be done in the open, and the negotiations were being piped live throughout the plant over the regular. P.A. system. Whenever Walesa made a particularly trenchant point, applause swelled up from outside. When Mieczyslaw Jagielski, the shrewd government negotiator, suggested at one point that because of time constraints they should hurry to sign the documents even though a few points remained to be resolved, jeers erupted outside and Walesa calmly declined. "Time?" he said. "Don't worry, we have time."

Meanwhile, outside the negotiating hall the strikers had commandeered the printing office and were hand-printing a daily newspaper, which they were passing between the bars of the closed gates to the throngs of townspeople gathered on the other side. Coming in the opposite direction, over the top of the wall, were vats of soup and loaves of bread. At night, the workers slept by their machines, their families having passed them blankets through the fence grille. The gate was slowly becoming festooned with flowers, crucifixes, and photos of the Pope. On Sunday morning, when the negotiations had reached a critical stage, a priest was brought in to say Mass. In the film, we watch a hush fall over the throngs on both sides of the gate, and everyone falls to his knees in silent prayer. Presently, they sing a religious hymn, and at this point a friend who was translating for me began to cry. "That hymn has been banned since the war," she whispered. "Look! Everyone still remembers the words."

During the negotiations, which covered twenty-one points, Walesa and his comrades were unmovable on the first two—the formation of an independent union and the right of that union to strike. When the government proved slow in acceding to another of the demands—the release of KOR advisers and other activists who had been herded up in recent days—Walesa warned that the strikers would not go back to work until the advisers were released, and that, once they were released, if any harm should come to them "we have an independent union and we retain our right to strike again."

The government negotiators were whipped; in the film they have the look of people who realize that the jig is up. In the large hall where the official signing ceremonies for the new covenant took place, a cross was conspicuously hanging on the wall between the Polish eagle and a sculpture of Lenin. Walesa signed the document with a huge souvenir pen commemorating the Pope's 1979 visit.

In Poland, the interpenetration of film and political reality is particularly fertile. Most Polish filmmakers start out as documentarians, even though many of their documentaries are shelved by the censor and never released. One result of the recent political developments has been a loosening of the censor's authority. Among the most popular film series in Warsaw these days is a retrospective of once-banned documentaries at Non-Stop Kino, entitled *From the Shelves.* Looking at some of these films, you get the feeling that if the Party leaders had taken the time to look at the documentaries their minions were busy banning they might have seen the current upheaval coming a mile away.

The day I went to Non-Stop, two efforts in particular stood out. Irina Kamienska's bleak portrait of women textile workers, *Robotnicy,* looked for all the world as if it had been shot in some Victorian hellhole amidst capitalist exploitation at its most savage: the relentless throb of the machinery, the dust-saturated air, the women wearing masks that both shield their lungs and muffle their voices. During one of their brief breaks, one particularly wrinkled and stooped old woman lets fall that she is in fact only forty years old.

Marcel Lozinski's darkly sardonic semi-documentary, *Proba Mikrofonu (Microphone Test),* is set inside a cosmetics factory where bored, alienated women run the endless assembly line. At one point the film's protagonist, the d.j. who's in charge of stocking the factory's P.A. system with spunky Muzak, gets it into his head to fashion an aural portrait of the women at the plant. He lugs his tape recorder around, asking the workers if they feel responsible for what's happening in the plant. Some say no, but most don't even know what he means by "responsible." From their puzzled reactions, he weaves a collage that he then tries to get approved by the factory's Party Central Committee. In the film's wry epilogue, the Committee members angrily denounce the whole project, insisting that "the workers don't know what they're talking about" and scolding the d.j. for asking the wrong questions ("If you had asked the proper questions, you would have known the answers in advance"). In the end the Committee votes to shelve the tape, just as upon Lozinski's completion of his project a few years ago, his own board of review voted to shelve the film.[4]

In a surprising number of Polish feature films, the fictional protagonist is a documentarian of some sort. In Krzysztof Kieslowski's *Amator (Camera Buff),* a factory worker acquires an 8-millimeter camera and gradually goes haywire, filming everything in sight, documenting life at home, in his plant, in the surrounding community, and eventually running afoul of the censor. In Janusz Kijowski's *Kung Fu,* a Warsaw journalist pursues a tangled thread of corruption and cover-up in a provincial manufacturing plant. In *Man of Marble,* Andrzej Wajda's 1977 masterpiece, and perhaps the most accomplished film in the genre, a young woman film student obsessively stalks the elusive trail of Birkut, a fictional "workers' hero" from the Stalinist fifties, a Stakhanovite brick mason whose awesome record at laying walls had catapulted him to national newsreel prominence, but who subsequently fell afoul of Stalinist purge trials and then disappeared. Through such documentarian protagonists, Polish directors during the late seventies seemed to be saying that in a corrupt and stagnant political situation it becomes a heroic task merely to discover and declare a true thing. As the years passed, that lucid insistence has recirculated through the Polish body politic, with sometimes surprising results.

When *Man of Marble* was released in 1977, it had clearly suffered a censor's slash. The last scenes, in which Agnieszka, the filmmaker, finally tracks down Birkut's son, Tomczyk, in the Gdansk shipyard, only to discover that Birkut himself died in the 1970 uprising, had been conspicuously mauled. Still, the film proved a tremendous success in Poland during 1978 and 1979; and in 1980, during the strike, when Wajda was visiting Gdansk, a shipworker shouted out to him, "Now you have to tell our story—*Man of Iron.*"

Wajda accepted the challenge. Perhaps no film-maker has been faced with this kind of national commission—this urgent mandate to fashion the onrush of lived and shared experience, as it is happening, into a mythic legacy—since the days of (of all people) Sergei Eisenstein. Wajda hired Chodakowski (fresh from *Robotnicy '80*) as his assistant director, and in a mere nine months they and their co-workers scripted, shot, and edited the new story—this one set against the climactic backdrop of the August events in Gdansk. In the new film, release of which still pended review by the Culture Ministry as of mid-May ("Hell," one director told me, "this one's going to have to be reviewed by the entire Central Committee!"), Winkiel, a washed-up, jaded, alcoholic journalist, receives a mysterious assignment to go to Gdansk and dig up any dirt he can find on Tomczyk—Birkut's son—who is one of the strike's ringleaders. Through flashbacks, we see Tomczyk's life—his student rage in 1968 when his father wouldn't join him, his own hesitation to join his father in 1970, his grief at his father's massacre, his work in the shipyards, his meeting with Agnieszka, their marriage, their work together in the activist underground, and the birth of their child. Much of the historical footage derives from a restaging of some of the haunting photos now on exhibit in Warsaw (most strikingly, the photo of the crowd surging forward, carrying the corpse on the door frame, from 1970); much of the Gdansk 1980 footage is lifted straight out of *Robotnicy '80.* The soundtracks of the strikes are actual, including that secret tape someone managed to preserve from the violence of 1970. Lech Walesa and Anna Walentynowicz make cameo appearances. In Poland today, filmmakers can conceive of nothing more compellingly dramatic than what is actually happening before their eyes. Fiction and documentary are merging in a new epic form.[5]

During the Gdansk strike in 1980, only one Party official emerged unscathed and if anything with higher stature in the eyes of most of the workers at the shipyard—Tadeusz Fiszbach, the Party boss in the Gdansk region. "He is the only one of those bastards who can sleep peacefully at night," a Solidarity leader told me in the yards. Indeed, this spring there was rumored to be an insurgent movement within the Party itself to place

Fiszbach at the head of the national Party at its coming summer congress. Anyway, Wajda invited Fiszbach to repeat his historic role in a cameo appearance in *Man of Iron,* and Fiszbach accepted the honor.

Polish cinema, which has had a good deal to do with generating the moral climate out of which the current political renewal has been emerging, is itself becoming one of that renewal's principal beneficiaries. During recent years, the Polish film industry reorganized itself into eight production units, each one headed by a world-class director (Wajda, for example, heads one unit, Zanussi another), who then represents his junior associates before the Culture Ministry in matters, for example, of funding and censorship. The Culture Ministry, however, had retained the right to veto production on specific projects.

In the early spring of this year, thanks to the liberalizing atmosphere, the production units extracted a new concession—the right under specific circumstances to veto the Culture Ministry's veto. The first test case of this new policy involves a fascinating script by a young screenwriter-director, Ryszard Bugajski, entitled *Preszuchanie (Cross Examination)*. This is the story of a defiant young woman held prisoner during the Stalinist witch-hunts of the early fifties; her rape by her examining magistrate; her pregnancy; his growing concern, confusion, and disintegration; and their daughter's activism, twenty years later, in an underground KOR publishing house. The script was summarily vetoed by the Culture Ministry during the winter, but this spring, Wajda, the head of Bugajski's unit, vetoed the veto.

"However," Bugajski told me one afternoon over drinks at the Hotel Forum, "this go-ahead is merely provisional. The economic crisis is forcing the political crisis, but it's also rendering some of the political gains somewhat moot. Today, for example, there are only thirty-five thousand metres of film stock in the entire country, for all the directors in Poland; and because of the foreign-exchange imbalance, we can't afford to buy any more."

Similarly, although censorship standards have eased on the importation of foreign films, Film Polski can't afford to bring any new films in. Roman Polanski, the Polish emigré director, was able to convince his producers to accept zlotys for their licensing of *Tess* in Poland, but nobody else in the world is going to accept Polish currency.

In publishing, likewise, new, more liberal standards have been formulated, but an extreme paper shortage means that it can take as long as three years for a book to get published in Poland. In Warsaw this May, you couldn't buy a Polish-English dictionary if your life depended on it; for that matter, Polish-Polish dictionaries were in short supply. "There's a sense in which the government and the Party are perfectly willing to extend us freedoms they know we can't use," a writer told me. "In a strange way, they have a vested interest in perpetuating the current economic constrictions."

In other fields, though, the economic crisis is abetting the spread of information. There may be a shortage of film stock, but there's also a shortage of videotape. Consequently the state television networks, which used to be the most zealously guarded and controlled media outlets, are having to turn more and more often to live coverage, with predictably spontaneous results. One afternoon, I joined a group of Poles outside a television store to watch live gavel-to-gavel coverage of the parliamentary debates over registration of the independent farmers' union—sessions whose results were by no means foregone. Few Poles used to take TV news seriously, but today most people watch—particularly the late-night broadcasts, where, like everyone else in Polish society, the TV newscasters seem to be testing the limits of their new situation. Details surface late at night which may disappear the next morning but will sometimes resurface several weeks later in prime time. Nobody quite knows the new rules. Poles watch TV partly for the news and partly for the news of what the news is allowed to say.

"It's crazy over there," a BBC reporter who was preparing a documentary on Polish television exclaimed to me over coffee one morning at the Hotel Victoria. "Television is supposed to be the Party's strongest bastion, but four thousand of the six thousand employees belong to Solidarity, admittedly mostly technicians and not the journalists—but *that* in itself presents interesting prospects. At some stage soon, Solidarity may be in a position to pull the plug on any coverage it finds offensive."

In some ways the most remarkable thing one finds in Poland these days is the breezy openness of political conversation. Indeed, Poland seems much more open politically today than does the United States—at least the Poles are *having* a political conversation. The constraints that until nine months ago limited all discourse appear to have melted away. While hard-liners in the Communist Party rail against "antisocialist elements" in the Solidarity movement, the latest craze on campus is a T-shirt emblazoned with the bold, Ben-Hur-like letters "EA," and underneath, in smaller typeface, the legend. "ELEMENTY ANTYSOCJALISTYCZNE." "Socialist? Antisocialist? Who knows what anyone means by those categories?" explains the enterprising T-shirt salesman. "People buy the shirts as a joke. If they want to call us that, fine—here, we'll wear it on our chest."

One afternoon I was in a hotel bar having an unusually frank political conversation with a screenwriter. At one point he nodded over his shoulder. "That guy over there," he whispered. "Police spy." I suggested that maybe we should move outside. "No, no," he insisted. "It's all right. Everything is open. Let him listen. Maybe he'll learn something."

Earlier this spring, in an exceptionally thoughtful passage in *The New Yorker*'s "Talk of the Town" section (April 13, 1981), the anonymous contributor noted that the real splendor of the current Polish renewal was the way it had, in one sudden surge, completely transcended the perennial revolutionary quandary about ends and means—about, for example, whether violence is an acceptable route to peace, or dictatorship to democracy. This contributor felt that the Poles had contrived a new strategy altogether:

> They appear to have discovered nothing less than a new principle of action. It is simply *to be what you want to become.* Thus, if you want to have free elections, begin by freely electing someone; if you want to have free speech, speak freely; if you want to have a trade union, found a trade union. The Poles have discovered that if enough people act in this way, the very foundations of the unwanted government begin to dissolve, even while it retains a monopoly on the means of violence.

And that has indeed been largely what has happened in the remarkable opening-out of Polish political discourse. Only, as I came to realize during my weeks in Poland, it didn't "just happen."

The Polish national renewal was preceded, over a period of several years, by countless acts of individual courage. This was particularly the case with the participants in KOR. One afternoon a writer showed me some back issues of KOR's *Biuletyn Informacyjny,* from the 1978-79 period, in which, on primitively mimeographed sheets, KOR had monitored the various campaigns of police harassment against activist workers on a case-by-case basis. In several issues, you can find accounts of the sporadic arrests and detentions of a Gdansk electrician named Lech Walesa. The thing that is particularly impressive about KOR's bulletin, however, is the fact that at the back of each issue the names, addresses, and phone numbers of the members of the KOR steering committee are openly provided (Jacek Kuron 39-39-64, Adam Michnik 28-43-55, etc.). It's as if KOR were calling out to everyone else, "Come on out! Be open. What can they do to us if we all start taking responsibility for our true dreams?"

One day I am introduced to Jan Litynski, a fortyish (Jewish) KOR activist, who started out as a mathematician but presently found himself editing *Robotnik,* one of the most vital of the post-1976 dissident journals. His English is extraordinarily good, considering that he's never been to England or America, and I ask him where he picked it up. "In jail," he answers, smiling. "That's where most of us learned our English. We had a lot of free time during the seventies."

I ask him if the transition to activism was frightening for him.

"The worst is the first time they throw you in jail without giving you any idea how long they're going to keep you," he replies. "I didn't know if I could stand that. It scared me. But I survived—one does—and afterward the fear was never so bad."

Because some people faced down that fear, the whole society today has opened out. And nowhere is that openness more breezy, more bracing than in Gdansk, the northern seaport where the repression started to come unravelled to begin with. The very first place the taxi-driver takes you when you arrive in the city provides the most bracing evidence of all. Just outside the gates of the Lenin Shipyard rises a towering, gleaming monument to the martyrs of December 16, 1970—a monument that nine months ago nobody would have thought possible, commemorating an event that nine months ago nobody official would even admit had happened. As part of the August 31, 1980, settlement, the shipworkers of Gdansk won the right to build a monument to their fallen comrades. For several years, each December 16th the plaza outside the shipyard entrance had become mysteriously strewn with commemorative wreaths. Now the shipworkers were intent on making sure that by December 16, 1980, the wreaths would adorn a proper altar. "And not some flat low slab of marble," the strikers insisted. "We want it to be visible from every place in the city!" And it is. The memorial was designed by Bogdan Pietruszka, one of the artisans in the shipyard; it was manufactured by the ship-workers themselves in a fever of activity in October and November, as if to mock the government's complaints about their low productivity. In early December, the three huge components were carried out of the shipyard into the plaza in an emotionally wrenching proces-sional: each component was a cross. The memorial con-sists of three towering crosses joined back to back at their arms in a triangular configuration. They rise a hundred and forty feet above the plaza. On their bases are bas-reliefs of workers erecting the memorial, work-ers at table with their families, and workers holding strike banners reading "SOLIDARNOSC." Gradually, these bas-reliefs give way to strong beams, piercing skyward. Crucified at the top are three anchors, their arms twisted in allegorical suffering.[6] The image is simple and yet tremendously powerful: it seems to gather up all the themes of the recent Polish experience. Along a fronting wall has been engraved a quotation from a Psalm translated by Czeslaw Milosz. My taxi-driver tells me that Milosz, whose books were banned in Po-land until recently, will visit the monument and the shipyards this June. While we are looking at the monu-ment, the afternoon shift lets out. Workers file through the gate, as they do every afternoon, and past these crosses, at once a memorial to their fallen comrades and a monument to their own remarkable vengeance. Some of them, as they pass, cross themselves across the chest.

Later that evening, while walking through the

quaint, exceptionally lovely old quarter of Gdansk, I begin to get a sense of another force that may have animated the 1980 rebellion. From almost anywhere in the city, the cranes of the shipyard dominate the skyline—huge, muscular limbs flexed toward heaven. These machines are absolutely mammoth: looming there, they suggest vast reserves of power, held in restraint through Olympian control. It's easy to see how a worker who spent his life around such machines might begin to have delusions of grandeur—how, when he lost patience with the pesky incompetent bureaucrats downtown, he just might begin to imagine he had the power to do something about them.

The next morning, I arrange an appointment with Stanislaw Bury, one of eleven members of the presidium of Solidarity's local chapter inside the Lenin Shipyard. On the way to the meeting (the Solidarity offices are just inside the main gate—workers pass them every day on their way in and out), I get a look at the bulletin board. On one poster, Article 19 of the Helsinki Agreements, dealing with human rights, is reproduced in full, and underneath it, in broad scrawl, is written, "Poland ratified this in 1977!" A faded poster features photos of the bloody, battered faces of two of the Solidarity leaders who were wounded in the Bydgoszcz incident back in March, with updates on their conditions and Solidarity's response. Another poster declares simply, "Monday through Friday we work for the Country—Saturday and Sunday are for you and your children."

Stanislaw Bury, a strong, roguish man in his late thirties, escorts me into his office. During our interview, people keep barging in, usually without knocking. That's one thing I notice everywhere I go in Solidarity: nobody bothers about honoring a closed door.

Bury explains his position in the union. At the time of the strike, he worked in the yards, but today, as a member of the shipyard local's presidium, he works full time for Solidarity. Each of the sixteen thousand ship-workers (and, for that matter, each of the ten million members of the national Solidarity) commits one per cent of his annual income to the union: sixty per cent of that is kept by the local chapter, and forty per cent goes to the national organization. The administrative functions of the local chapter are handled by the presidium, two of whose eleven members—Lech Walesa and Anna Walentynowicz—in practice spend all their time across town, at the national headquarters. The presidium is elected from among a ninety-four-member council of delegates, who, in turn, are elected by the membership through the local's subdivisions. The presidium meets as a body every day, the council once a week. The presidium is answerable to the council on all issues, and only the council can render final decisions. Each week, the ninety-four delegates pass along complaints and comments from their constituents, and at the beginning of each council meeting the presidium has to report on actions it has taken in response to the previous week's concerns. All delegates and presidium members are elected for two-year terms, with a maximum consecutive service of four years, and they are subject to immediate recall at any time.

Bury points out that a special regulation requires that at the end of their terms the presidium members must return to the yard with exactly the job they had upon joining the presidium, and they cannot then accept advancements for at least one year. "We are still young at this," Bury explains. "Nine months—hardly even a toddler yet. We are still trying to learn how to make democracy work. It's very hard, and we have no experience. But we are making improvements. For example, we now have a rule that final passage of any item by the council of delegates requires a three-fourths majority vote. We feel that if we haven't achieved that level of consensus we haven't considered the issue long enough."

Each of the nine active presidium members supervises a specifically apportioned territory besides handling general tasks. One supervises internal finances, one supervises elections, one attends to individual grievances, one is developing the groundwork for a workers' council with the collaboration of "experts," one does troubleshooting . . . "Me," Bury says, smiling, "I'm in charge of propaganda."

I ask Bury if he sees any application at the national level of the lessons in democratic process which they've acquired locally.

"Oh," he says, sighing. "You're asking too much. We are only just beginning to understand horizontal democracy. Vertical democracy will be a labor of many years."

At the conclusion of our interview, I ask Bury whether he could give me a tour of the shipyard itself. In the meantime, a few other Westerners have gathered in the hall—a Canadian historian, a Swedish student leader, an American lawyer—and they all join in the request.

An assistant starts to explain that the yard is a security installation, off limits to—

"Nonsense," Bury interrupts. "If they're with me, there's no problem."

We leave the office and head for the yard, walking right past the guards, who merely nod cheerfully toward Bury. It turns out that even the guards belong to Solidarity.

We pass all the places I'd seen a few days earlier in *Robotnicy '80*—the entry plaza where Sunday Mass had been held, the hall where the delegations from other factories had listened in on the negotiations, and, off to the side, the small room where the negotiations themselves had worn on and on. Everywhere in the yard, we pass beneath the large speakers of the P.A. system, speakers that in August broadcast the negotiations live. Usually they confine themselves to upbeat pop melodies; today, however, they are offering somber, elegiac classical and religious music—the wounded Pope is still in very serious condition. Every few minutes an authoritative voice announces a special 6 P.M. Mass in the main cathedral.

I don't know why, but I never really enjoyed the Socialist Realism that permeates so much of the old American left's depiction of the Pride of the Workers: the kind of thing you find a lot of in "socially conscious" movies from the thirties and forties—all that determined brawn and those broad smiles. But that's what it actually feels like in the Gdansk shipyard. These workers are *proud.* They walk around as if they mattered: they've really proved themselves, and nobody'd better mess with them again. Especially Bury himself. He ambles around, greeting just about everyone, slowing down to listen to complaints or offer updates on grievances, to accept invitations to weddings or to jokingly chide one worker on his poor attendance at meetings— he struts around as if he *owned* the place. And in a way he does. He and his fellow-organizers, who just a year ago were having to meet in secret and endure endless harassments, are today clearly the authoritative force in the yard.

All around us, huge tankers and container ships are coming into being. At one point, we pass a puny little yacht, incongruously shackled to a dock. I ask Bury about it.

"Confiscated," he says. "Used to belong to the head of the state TV network."

I ask him if he thinks that he and his comrades have been building better ships since Aug—

"Yes!" He doesn't even let me finish the sentence.

It's all quite exhilarating, this walk among the workers. But it's also profoundly disheartening, because, for all their pride, these men and women are laboring at backbreaking jobs under horrible conditions (in one hangar, the brown air hangs suspended, it seems, al-

most in clots)—conditions that have not changed over-
night and are not about to change significantly any
time soon.

Poland is a poor, poor country, and this is going to
have to be a long, slow revolution.

One "Western source," as he preferred to have himself characterized, during a "deep background" session
I'd had a few days earlier in Warsaw noted, "There is,
of course, an exhilaration in all this venting of anger,
but at some point the economic reality of Poland's situation is going to require some extraordinary maturity
on the part of Solidarity's leadership. They've shown
they can take the nation out on strike, but can they put
it back to work? Specifically, they are going to have to
motivate workers to a much higher productivity while
at the same time prevailing upon them to accept a siz-
able cut in their already low standard of living, at least
over the short term. It took American unions forty years
to reach that level of maturity; it's asking a lot of a year-
old organization."

My Western source's celebration of the relative maturity of American labor struck me as ironic. Two
weeks earlier, back in the States, I had asked William
Winpisinger, the head of the International Association
of Machinists & Aerospace Workers, which is one of the
leading industrial unions in America, what he felt
American labor could teach Solidarity.

"Hell, it's the other way around," he replied. "It's
what they can teach us. For instance, they can teach us
balls. While American labor has been steadily back-
tracking on all fronts, Solidarity has reminded us what
spine is all about. And they've done it by uniting: shipworkers, truckers, coal miners, secretaries, machinists—
everyone uniting around a set of general principles.
American labor today lacks principle as a movement.
And until American labor and the American left generally learn to fashion that kind of solidarity on behalf of

principle, we're going to continue to be the pathetic victims of our American bosses, just as much as, until recently, the Poles were the victims of theirs."

The question remains, however: Just what is Solidarity's plan for the nation? Sometimes Solidarity's aspirations seem very large indeed. According to a banner at the entrance to the Lenin Shipyard, "THE GOVERNMENT TAKES CARE OF LAWS, THE PARTY TAKES CARE OF POLITICS, AND SOLIDARITY TAKES CARE OF THE NATION." But when you talk to individual union officials the answers are often considerably more circumspect.

"Up to now, we've avoided taking economic responsibility," a staff member at the Warsaw Solidarity office once explained to me, addressing my Western source's concerns more directly. "The government has recently been trying to maneuver us into taking some form of co-responsibility in areas such as productivity, but we've declined to do so until we can fashion mechanisms whereby we can exert substantial leverage in formulating and carrying out economic policy."

Sometimes answers can get downright coy. "They got us into this mess, let them get us out," Bury said the day we spoke in his Gdansk office. "Besides, we're workers, not economists."

That abrupt response notwithstanding, Solidarity is intensely interested in the future of economic life in Poland—it's just that it is taking longer for an economic consensus to emerge than it did for the political consensus. Or, to phrase it more precisely, an overwhelming number of Poles have an astonishingly consistent idea of what they don't like in their lives—the distant and arbitrary central authority, the repression, the corruption. They also have a consensus, in general terms, on what they want to replace it with: some sort of democratic worker control in the workplace. But when you get to asking specific questions about what that democratic control will look like, what the workers will democratically choose to do with that control, and how the pieces will fit together, things get very hazy. It's just too soon to tell. And, in the absence of consensus on such precise issues, Solidarity is taking its time.

In a sparsely furnished office at the union's nondescript national headquarters, in Gdansk, I meet Bogdan Lis, the vice-chairman of Solidarity and Lech Walesa's first lieutenant. Lis looks tired—his expression is haggard. He looks like he has been bearing the weight of the world on his shoulders for months, and in a way he has. His hair is thinning, maybe even beginning to gray. I ask him how old he is, and he replies, twenty-eight. (Walesa is thirty-seven. Andrzej Gwiazda, the old man of the union leadership, is forty-five. Zbigniew Brjak, the head of the union's Warsaw region branch, Solidarity's largest, is twenty-five. Jerzy Borowczak, who was one of the main firebrands during the Gdansk strike and is now a leader on the shipyard-union presidium, has just turned twenty-one.) As exhausted as Lis seems, he still clearly revels in the play of words and silences which so often characterizes an official Solidarity interview. The way some people have worry lines, Bogdan Lis has developed irony lines: they crinkle out from his eyes whenever he feels the need to turn orphic, and he's a master. When he's asked about the Soviet Union, for instance, his face opens into a wry smile that speaks volumes without leaving a quotable trace. "Are you kidding?" his eyes seem to say. "You think I'm going to jeopardize all this for some easy quip? Next question, please."

I ask Lis about the distinction between "political" and "social" realms that seems at the heart of so much of the ongoing wordplay between the government and the union. The government accuses the union of trying to become "political," while the union insists that it's continuing to be merely "social."

"That goes back to the August agreements," Lis explains. "Late in the bargaining, something very interesting happened. The Party has long considered itself to be the leading force in all political and social affairs in this country. In the early drafts of the agreement, there was language to that effect in the text—it basically echoed similar formulations in the state constitution—in which the union agreed that the Party would continue to play such a role. At one point, however, late in the negotiations, when all kinds of other things were going on, we merely deleted the words 'and social' from the formulation—and they never noticed! They signed a document in which all we conceded was the Party's leading role 'in political matters'—and, of course, we still concede that." The irony lines blossom across his face once again.

The game really comes into its own when you try to get a union official to specify which issues are "social" and which "political," and this is one of Bogdan Lis's specialties. "The media, for instance, are social institutions," he says. "And therefore Solidarity has every right to demand an end to state censorship. The improvement of working conditions is a social issue, as is the appropriate distribution of wealth throughout the society. For that matter, the liberation of political prisoners is also a social issue."

"Well, then, what's a political issue?"

"Why, the sort of thing the Party concerns itself with." [7]

Similarly, Solidarity spokesmen often contrast legal authority, which they admit they lack, with moral authority, which they insist they have—the implication being, of course, that the legal authorities lack moral authority and are, indeed, immoral. A few days later, back in Warsaw, I happen to be watching television with a Polish friend. A Communist Party official is complaining that Solidarity wants to reduce the Party's role to that of a discussion club. "No," my friend says. "He's got it all wrong. The role we have in mind for the

Party is something a bit more like that of the British queen."

In Poland today, Solidarity officials insist that they speak on behalf of "society." Over and over, one hears such phrases as "The society wants this" and "The society won't stand for that." And most of the people one talks to in the street concur: not only is Solidarity their representative, it is the expression of Polish society. I have heard several Solidarity spokesmen scoff at the government's accusations that they are anti-socialist. "On the contrary," they insist, "socialism consists in the *social* ownership of the means of production, which is *precisely* what we advocate."

This last word game, however, yields a kernel of substantive significance—because although Solidarity (and society) may not yet have arrived at a consensus on how to proceed from here, there is virtually no one in Poland who advocates the restitution of a capitalist free market. "There is a profound egalitarian impulse at the heart of the Solidarity movement," explains a Warsaw sociologist who has spent time in the West. "Maybe that's one valuable legacy of the thirty-five years of Communist rule here: people have been exposed to those slogans for so long that now they want to make them real. There has thus far been relatively little individual opportunism. The movement's first concern has been for its poorest members. Wage demands, for instance, have always been on an across-the-board rather than a percentage basis. Everybody, no matter what his current salary, gets an extra thousand zlotys rather than an extra five per cent.[8] As a researcher, I have no objection to seeing a factory worker get paid more than I do; after all, I enjoy my work, while his is often drudgery. And I think my attitude is fairly common among professionals here in Poland. I think I'd be hard pressed, though, to find a similar attitude among professionals in the West."

During my last few days in Poland, the cigarette shortage gets serious. Everybody in Poland seems to smoke. "You would, too, if you'd been living here the last nine months," an acquaintance tells me teasingly. By the end of the week, you can't buy a pack anywhere. Even the PEWEX shops have run out. And yet, on innumerable occasions, I see people go up to complete strangers, ask for a cigarette, and get one. I see people with two cigarettes left in their last pack not hesitate for a moment to offer one of them to the most casual of acquaintances. It seems that each person knows that when his pack runs out he'll be able to borrow from the next, and that there will be no hoarding. The country will just share until the shortage has exhausted itself. The only trouble is, nobody has any matches.

In *The Road to Gdansk,* a remarkable book on recent Polish history which was completed a mere six weeks before the onset of the August, 1980, strike in Gdansk, Daniel Singer, one of the most insightful chroniclers of the situation in Eastern Europe, concluded:

> The tensions are such that nobody in Warsaw asks whether everything will blow up once again, but when it will happen. The crucial question is whether the explosion can be put off sufficiently to allow for the emergence of a political movement, resting on real social forces, strong enough to move beyond veto power to impose changes in policies and institutions, but also cohesive enough and sufficiently in charge of the situation to dissuade the Russians from taking the plunge. It is difficult to be very optimistic about this race against the clock.

Singer's trepidation notwithstanding, the Solidarity movement during its first nine months has performed

extraordinarily well precisely with regard to the criteria
that Singer set. Most Poles I have spoken with were
as pleasantly surprised by the movement's cohesion,
strength, and maturity as Singer must be.[9] But now the
questions are beginning to change. It seems to me that
today they fall into three general areas: (1) How, specifically, even under ideal conditions, does a body politic
begin to mesh its desire for a decentralized system of
democratic worker control of the workplace with its
need for some kind of integrated national planning?
(There are no models here. No one in modern history
has succeeded in mastering this challenge.) (2) How,
specifically, given the realities of Polish political life
today but for the moment excluding the question of the
country's economic situation, can Solidarity move to
carry out some of its policies while avoiding any direct
confrontation with the Communist Party, on the one
hand, and the huge, entrenched bureaucracy, on the
other? What will the distribution of power in Poland
look like two years from now? And, finally (3), given
Poland's actual economic situation, are any of these
reforms happening in time? Is it already too late to
salvage the foundering Polish economy? To phrase the
question a bit differently, will the economic realities
allow the Poles any room to maneuver? To phrase it
more darkly, are all the things that are happening in
Poland today merely epiphenomena—lots of dazzle and
firecrackers that blind us to the essential reality, which
is that the country is going bankrupt and all forms of
authority are therefore melting away? Do we have any
idea what it means for a semi-developed country to go
bankrupt in 1981? —what happens next? While almost
all the Poles I spoke with expressed enthusiastic support
for the Solidarity movement, many were quietly skepti-
cal of the movement's long-term chances. Their misgivings almost always centered on this third area.

One thing that most Poles I spoke with were *not*
worrying about in May, 1981, was the possibility of a

Soviet invasion. Over and over Poles asked me about "the hysterical concern of the Western media over this question of whether the Soviets will invade."

"Some of the American reporters here in Gdansk have been so busy looking out to sea waiting for the Soviet armada," one Solidarity staffer complained, "that they've hardly even noticed what we've been doing in the yards."

"Well," another corrected him, "actually, most of the really hysterical stories have been datelined Washington or New York or Paris. The reporting out of here has usually been fairly decent."

"It's almost as if the Western media and the U.S. State Department *wanted* the Soviets to invade," one screenwriter commented. "As if what we are trying to do here were in some way as threatening to corporate capitalism as it is to Soviet-style Communism." [10]

Have the Poles themselves worried at any point about a Soviet invasion?

"That was not one of our main concerns," another writer told me. "There were maybe four days last March, at the height of the Bydgoszcz crisis"—when Solidarity brought the nation to the brink of a general strike by protesting a brutal police attack on three of its regional leaders—"when the Warsaw Pact forces were dragging their maneuvers on and on. For a few days there, yes, it was very tense, there were even rumors that the Soviets had streaked a few of their jets over Warsaw as part of the maneuvers, and that rattled our nerves pretty good. But at a certain point, after they kept threatening and threatening and threatening and *not* acting—well, the threat began to wear thin. Each new threat proved that they were even more scared than we were."

When I asked Poles what they would do if the Soviets did invade, I got a variety of answers. Some said they would fight, some said they would fight if others fought (when I asked where they would get the arms, they assured me that the Army would provide them, the Army, after all, being made up largely of conscripts, which is to say, of their brothers and their friends), some said they would simply refuse to work, and some said that there were ways of causing damage without specifically resorting to arms. But perhaps the most trenchant reply came from a man in a Gdansk bar: "O.K., so they invade. So what? We will simply go on doing what we're doing. To stop us, they'd have to send in one Soviet soldier for every Pole, and if they did that, one by one, one on one, we'd convert their entire Army."

"Look," another man at the bar said. "The Russians are no longer allowing any of their citizens to get tourist visas to visit Poland, or Poles to get visas to visit Russia. You think they're going to go and expose four hundred thousand of their young, impressionable future workers to what's going on here?"

The more time you spend in Poland, the more irrelevant the Soviet Army seems. After a while, the question of a Soviet invasion just seems beside the point. As you line up the arguments for and against such an invasion from the Soviet point of view, such a strategy appears transparently counterproductive. Having said that, one should also note that recent history provides no particular ground for deeming temperate consideration one of the principal characteristics of top-level planning in either of the superpowers. Still, it should be clear that, given the extremely constricted economic situation in Poland today, the Soviet Union finds itself with all kinds of opportunities for leverage without having to resort to outright invasion. To say that an invasion is unlikely, therefore, is not to dismiss the significance of the Soviet factor.

Thus the Poles come hurtling back toward summer, the first anniversary of their remarkable resurgence. All over Poland, people are looking toward the immediate future, toward what promises to be an extremely eventful few months: the Communist Party convocation has been set for July and will be preceded by a wide-open round of grass-roots balloting. By late August or early September, if it has the time to pull it together, Solidarity hopes to hold its first national convention, with delegates elected from all over the country in balloting that will in one way or another involve all ten million members. With the Polish primate, Cardinal Wyszynski, lying near death, the Catholic Church may likewise be experiencing a major period of transition. Czeslaw Milosz will be returning from exile in June to accept an honorary doctorate from the Catholic University in Lublin, and then he will visit the shipyard in Gdansk. In one form or another, Wajda's film "Man of Iron" should be opening. Meanwhile, on the stage, another returning exile, Roman Polanski, will be appearing as the naughty-boy genius Mozart in his own production of Peter Shaffer's *Amadeus*.

"You have no idea how things have changed," the filmmaker Ryszard Bugajski tells me one afternoon in Warsaw. "Today, you see all this activity, all this energy. At the beginning of last summer, there was so much depression, so much hopelessness. It wasn't even like hitting your head against a brick wall. Rather, it was like running up against a wall of butter—it gave a little, but never enough, and in the meantime you got all sticky and soiled. Now, at least, things are tangible—the challenge is solid."

On the eve of my departure from Poland, at a coffee-shop in Warsaw, I ask a staff member from the regional Solidarity office how long she thinks the reforms can continue, how far they can reach, whether there is a line that the Poles will not possibly be allowed to cross.

"We crossed that line," she replies, without a moment's hesitation, "back in August, 1980."

The Polish Airlines morning flight for East Berlin, scheduled to leave at 11:45, in fact leaves at 9:45. If you happen to be at the airport, you've got yourself a ride.

The Polish customs officials in Warsaw clear my luggage without even a cursory inspection. An hour and a half later, my plane lands at East Berlin's Schoenfeld International; I am intending, following customs, to bus the mere quarter-mile into West Berlin. The East German customs officials, however, noting my American passport and Warsaw point of origin, escort me into a small, bare, fluorescent-lit room. There they summarily empty my bags and in no time divulge some Solidarnosc posters, pins, and, presently, the photos of the 1970 massacre that the young man in Gdansk gave me for safekeeping. The junior agents quickly summon their superiors, and over the next forty-five minutes, virtually all the customs people at Schoenfeld parade in to examine the material. They grill me with questions, to which I feign naive incomprehension. After an hour my predicament begins to feel fairly serious; but just as I am beginning to wonder about the applicability of my Miranda rights and whether *they* supply the dime, it becomes evident that my interrogators aren't so much officially angry as personally curious. They, too, want to know what is going on in Poland.

INTERLUDE

A few weeks later, back in the United States, I happen to recall an old Polish joke, vintage early seventies. "What nationality were Adam and Eve?" the wag would ask you, and you'd say you didn't know, and he'd say, "Polish," and you'd ask, "Why?"

"Well," he'd say thoughtfully, "for three reasons." And then he'd list them. "First off, they were so poor they couldn't afford any clothes and had to run around naked. Second, between them, all they had to eat was one apple. And third, *they thought they were in paradise!*"

And you'd laugh, or you wouldn't. But the point is that that joke, which used to be merely derogatory—one more swipe at the supposed stupidity of "the Pollacks"—has in the meantime undergone an extraordinary transformation: it has become purely descriptive.

Part Two
SEPTEMBER–OCTOBER 1981

Four months have passed and I am back in Warsaw, Poland, in September, 1981. Paradise in fall. Paradise fallen.

One of the first things I come upon here in Warsaw is a slightly defaced wall poster advertising the new season of Poland's famous national circus, Cyrk. The poster reads:

CYRK
presents
A new, action-packed 1981 season
featuring
Trained animals, dogs, horses,
acrobats, jugglers, clowns and
countless other attractions.

Beside the "CYRK" someone has scrawled, in plain black letters, "POLSKA."
Circus Poland.

But no one is laughing, and the vitality has gone out of life in Poland this sorry autumn.

Elsewhere, the city is plastered with posters for Andrzej Wajda's film *Man of Iron,* which opened, uncensored, during the summer and is playing to packed houses. (Virtually everyone I speak with has seen the film at least once.) There are two posters. In one, a blood-smeared long-sleeved white shirt is spread-eagled against a plain white backdrop—a reference to the crucifixion of Poland's red-and-white flag during the events of 1970. The other poster alludes to the events of 1980, and shows the head of a large, powerful worker. An oversize metal industrial nut has been wedged around his temples, and as his facial muscles strain in grim determination the nut is splitting apart. (Wajda himself has been down in Krakow directing a stage production of *Hamlet,* what one might call Shakespeare's version of *Man of Iron*—another tale about legitimacy and false succession, in which the hero avenges the murder, by a counterfeit pretender, of his father, the state's rightful ruler.)

There are other posters, of course. One shows a skull and crossbones—or, more accurately, a skull and crossed fork and knife. It's captioned "THE FIRST RESULT OF THE COMMUNIST PARTY'S NINTH CONGRESS: LOWER FOOD RATIONS." The poster is often taped on shopwindows; its vacant eye sockets stare back at the vacant faces in the lines.[11]

The shelves in the shops are even emptier than they were during my last visit, in May, the lines much longer. Sporadic shortages have given way to pervasive insufficiencies in almost every sector of the economy. One of the most extreme shortages on the list—and one that is causing particular consternation and anxiety among the Poles—is soap. Only fresh vegetables and certain fruits seem plentiful; September, after all, is the peak of a rather good harvest season. The produce is brought in privately by farmers from the surrounding

countryside—they bypass the official government purchasing centers and sell in outdoor public markets, at
several times the official price. Jan Kulaj, the head of
Rural Solidarity—the agricultural union—recently told
an interviewer from Solidarity's *Glos Wolny,* "Except for
meat and citrus fruit, there shouldn't be any shortages
of food in Poland now. I want to tell you that in my
district alone hundreds of thousands of tons of cucum-
bers, cabbage, and other products were squandered because of the inefficiency of purchasing centers."

Although the per-capita income has gone up twenty-
seven per cent during the last year, thanks mostly to
Solidarity's agitation, the cost of living has risen much
faster for most Poles. Just how much faster is difficult to
determine, because so much of the inflation is hidden.
There are the official price increases—cigarettes, for example, up almost a hundred per cent; a loaf of bread up
two hundred per cent—but these provoke such resistance that the government tends to just leave prices as
they are and let supplies lapse. To phrase it more char-
itably, the government cannot afford to deliver products at the price that people demand and lacks the
legitimacy to raise prices to a more realistic level; therefore, it simply stops attempting to meet the demand.
People are left to scramble for themselves, outside official channels—in a market where their ration cards are
useless and prices are seemingly without limit. Indeed,
some farmers have stopped selling their produce altogether: the zloty being worthless, they prefer to deal
exclusively by barter—and few city dwellers have anything the farmers would be willing to trade for.

The situation is made for profiteering. In one increasingly common practice, a trucker bringing, say, twenty
thousand zlotys' worth of meat to market gives the
storekeeper twenty thousand zlotys (perhaps a bit
more) in cash and then sells the meat on the black
market at a five-hundred-per cent markup. "The government's not satisfied with having wrecked our econ-

omy," a disgusted shopper tells me. "Now it has to give us a Mafia, too."

Rationing, far from stabilizing the economy, as Solidarity had hoped it would early in the crisis when the union demanded its imposition, has introduced some destabilizing elements of its own. The rationing system is administered on a regional basis, with the result that neighboring districts may have wildly different allocations: places that have plentiful milk coupons may not have milk, whereas the next village may face the opposite situation. There seems to be little relationship between the number of coupons issued and the anticipated supply of a given product. Meanwhile, many people who have been denied government-sanctioned employment aren't allotted any coupons at all for such basics as sugar, butter, and meat. Once again, the result is a highly inflationary black market—this time in the coupons for regular food.

"Rationing *or* lines," a woman standing outside a grocery store comments. "You expect one or the other, but not both at the same time. And then to have the price increases on top of that. It's really too much."

Over and over, older Poles offer the same eerie comparison: "Take a look," they say, showing you their ration cards. "Now go look up the figures. These allotments are even lower than in Nazi times!"

A particularly hard situation is faced by families with alcoholic members—of which there are distressingly many. The standard ration for vodka is now only half a litre a month. With two coupons, you can buy a standard litre bottle for a few hundred zlotys—if you can find the bottle. People intent on getting more must either go to a restaurant or bar, where a litre bottle can cost upward of a thousand zlotys, or trade the meat, milk, bread, and other portions of their family's coupon cards for vodka stamps. "Either way," someone tells me, "those families are beginning to starve."

Long before 1980, you could get certain goods only at

government-run PEWEX stores, and only for dollars or other hard currencies. But as the value of the zloty plummets, it takes more and more zlotys to buy the same number of dollars, and hence the same items at the PEWEX stores. Just how many more can be seen any day of the week outside the Hotel Forum, where the black-market rate of exchange for a single dollar (the official rate is now around thirty-four zlotys to the dollar [12]) has leapt from a hundred and sixty zlotys in May to between three hundred and three hundred and forty zlotys four months later. (Black market computations are therefore a bit easier on this trip: factors of ten. The street value of the dollar has ballooned to approximately ten times the official rate!)

You want to know how bad the economic situation is in Poland today? Well, there is a coin, an actual piece of metal, called the grosz, one hundred of which equal one zloty. It would take you three hundred of these coins—a treasure trove—to buy one American penny.

The 1973 and 1979 oil crises in the United States forced Americans to wade through some moderately long lines, but those crises lapsed within a few weeks, and the lines quickly disappeared. Imagine a situation in which you have to queue up not only for gasoline (for which the average wait in Warsaw is now two hours) but also for food, appliances, clothes, soap—just about everything—and that you have been doing so for months: imagine that, and you begin to sense what daily life is like in Poland today. Now imagine that supplies are clearly dwindling and winter is coming on.

Perhaps the biggest difference between September and May isn't the size and length of the lines but the spirit of the people in them. Back in May, the lines were friendly places where neighbors gathered, at the beginning or end of their day, to share gossip or trade opinions about political developments. People aren't talking in the lines anymore: the faces are grim, and fistfights are not infrequent. During this visit, I notice, as I perhaps failed to last time, the high number of young children in the lines—two- and three-year-olds. Most young women seem to have toddlers in tow. (More than half the population of Poland today is under thirty, and three million Poles, out of a total population of thirty-five million, are less than four years old.) It isn't so much that the Poles have large families; their Catholicism notwithstanding, as I mentioned before, most families seem limited to two or three children. Rather, it simply seems that in Poland, as opposed to America, the postwar baby-boom generation has been getting married fairly young and having a baby boom of its own—or was having one until recently. On this trip, I haven't noticed many pregnant women or many infants under six months of age. "Women who have babies today are the heroes of this country," a friend tells me. There is an extreme shortage of milk.

Even the luxury restaurants catering to tourists and the upper levels of Poland's bureaucratic bourgeoisie are noticeably straining now. At the Bazyliszek, perhaps the poshest restaurant in Warsaw, the offerings are confined to wild game—boar, stag, wild duck. There's no beef available. At most restaurants, if you ask for chicken they'll say, "No, you're having pork"— or vice versa, depending on the vagaries of available supply. At my hotel restaurant in Gdansk, my waiter and I play this game for about a week, but no matter what he claims to be bringing—"chicken," "pork," "veal," "lamb"—he always ends up delivering the same patty of nondescript ground-up flesh; only the sauces vary. Toward the end of my stay in Warsaw, access to the restaurant at the Hotel Forum, which somehow manages to keep up its "intercontinental" standard, is suddenly being restricted to hotel guests.

"It's really tragic," one American tourist, a veteran of many Polish vacations in better times, says to me one afternoon. "Poland has an exceptional national cuisine, and there are some extraordinary chefs in this country.

You know how they've set up preserves for wild African animals in the United States, for instance, to protect them from the political chaos in their home countries, with the hope that someday they'll be able to return them to their natural habitats? Well, somebody ought to do the same thing with Polish chefs."

Many things that were available only for hard currency back in May are no longer available at all. A moderately well-off friend tells me that he has been trying to procure motor oil for his car for two months and hasn't seen any anywhere—not even at the PEWEX shops. He's worried that he'll soon run his car into the ground and then be forced to rely on public transport. For that matter, buses have been breaking down at an alarming rate for lack of proper maintenance and spare parts—in other words, for lack of hard currency. Routes which used to be serviced every ten minutes are now lucky to see a bus once an hour; when the buses do arrive, they're often too packed to take on new passengers. Most queues seem to be attached to buildings or shops; when you see an apparently free-floating line milling by the roadside, it generally means that a bus is long overdue. "Millions of zlotys went into transportation during the past ten years," a man standing in one such line tells me. "But most of it went into highway construction. Gierek didn't care about anyone who couldn't afford a car."

Some of the longest lines in Warsaw these days spill out of the visa section of the Western embassies. You think it's hard getting into Poland from the United States, you should try going the other way around. "We get about two hundred applications for tourist visas every day," one American embassy official tells me, "about sixty per cent which we reject right off because the applicants clearly cannot demonstrate touristic intent." (Among Poles, the West German embassy has a reputation of being somewhat more lenient.)

"That does it," an American businessman friend of

mine says one afternoon when the driver of the taxi we are sharing parks his car by the roadside, opens his trunk, pulls out three jerry cans of gasoline, and begins filling his tank. "That does it. Now I have seen *every* image of life the way it was being lived in Europe when I was a soldier stationed in Germany right after the war. The jerry cans, the lines, the black market in currency, the ration cards, the desperation for chocolates and nylons, the prostitutes, the crowds milling round the embassies trying to get visas—it's as if the war ended here just six months ago."

And although Bob Dylan has been replaced in the Muzak at the Hotel Forum by Gloria Gaynor singing her gutsy disco paean, "I Will Survive" (it is a song you hear everywhere in Poland this fall, coming in over taxicab radios or hummed at nearby tables in student cafés), survival seems a decidedly open question.

Indeed, the three questions with which I left Poland back in May now seem to have been superseded by a fourth, far more urgent one: How the hell is this country going to make it at all through the coming winter?

One evening in early September, rumors spread throughout Poland—rumors that were presently being corroborated by hastily printed Solidarnosc fact sheets slapped onto public walls—concerning a prison take-over in Bydgoszcz, a town about eighty miles south of Gdansk. The prisoners, protesting conditions in the jail, had taken over the yard; the guards and city police were surrounding the prison; the people of Bydgoszcz were surrounding the guards; the power of the Polish state was surrounding the people of Bydgoszcz; the eyes of the Polish nation were constraining the power of the Polish state; the military might of the Soviet Union and the Warsaw Pact was threatening the vigilance of the Polish nation; and the concern of the West was limiting the options for exercise of Soviet might.

It was another instance of what was becoming a classic pattern in post-1980 Poland. For a few hours we all held our breath: Don't Anybody Move.

Eventually the prisoners surrendered—but to Solidarity, not to their guards.

I spoke about the incident the next day with John Darnton, the *New York Times* correspondent. He recounted a conversation he'd had several months earlier with a man who has since become a high government and Party official. "What you have to remember about this country," the man had said, "is that the whole society hates the authorities, the society wants to overthrow the authorities, the society has the power to overthrow the authorities—*and the society cannot overthrow the authorities.*"

Darnton's wife, Nina, who is a correspondent for National Public Radio, told me the same story from another angle. "A few months back," she recalled, "I was present when Adam Michnik, one of the leaders of KOR, went to a factory where he was going to address the workers. It was during a stage when a lot of emphasis was being put on the workers' political education. Some of them started complaining about the incompetence and corruption of the plant's managers, and Michnik very thoughtfully and carefully tried to raise the discussion to a higher level—'to raise their consciousness,' as it were. He explained that it wasn't merely a problem of individual personalities—that the system itself bred such distortions, that they could replace those managers with other people, but that because of the system, those new people would behave similarly . . . Suddenly, one of the workers shouted, 'Right! So let's get rid of the whole system!' Michnik immediately had to double back and explain that— well, there were certain geopolitical realities that had to be taken into account, and that you couldn't just . . . And so on."

In many ways, the situation in Poland seems con-

stantly on the verge of stalemate: each of the sides—
Solidarity, the Party, the Soviet Union—has the power
to veto the initiatives of any of the others but lacks the
power to push its own program through. (I include the
Soviet Union in this formulation because perhaps
the most fundamental element in the whole remarkable
situation is that the Soviet Union, for all its military
and economic leverage, has not been able to impose its
will, and doesn't seem likely to be able to any time
soon.) The result is that periods of intense, often perverse, and sometimes terrifying bickering are occasionally suspended for moments of wary, and then often
short-lived, compromise.

In Poland today, the institution with power lacks
legitimacy, while the institution with legitimacy lacks
power. Or, as Jan Litynski, a veteran KOR activist, put it
to me, "In this country today, there are two powers and
no power."

There had been some hope back in July that the
Communist Party could transcend this near-deadlock
by renewing itself in the public's estimation. There was
at the time much emphasis—perhaps more in the West
than in Poland itself—on the supposedly democratic
character of the delegate-selection process for the
Party's national congress and the surprisingly open
character of the floor debate. "I guess it was after the
Party congress that my gloom really bottomed out," a
Western diplomat in Warsaw told me in early September. "I mean, the only way I can see this logjam breaking is if both sides, Solidarity and the Communist
Party, develop strong, authentic leadership—two leadership bodies capable of sitting down for some hard,
solid negotiating and then of delivering on the terms of
those negotiations. We have yet to see if Solidarity itself
will come up with that kind of leadership, but it's pretty
much a moot point, because the Party didn't. Some of
the faces changed—surprisingly few—but the leadership
that emerged can hardly be considered strong, either

in authenticity or in imagination. The few strong, imaginative people (people like Tadeusz Fiszbach of Gdansk) didn't make the final cut, because the two extremes at the congress tended to cancel each other out, leaving only this fairly mediocre middle."

"Oh, the Party congress was very democratic," a Gdansk taxi-driver assured me. "It's a party of idiots, and they elected the biggest idiots as their leaders."

At the time of the Gdansk strike, in August of 1980, one of the most succinct bits of graffiti, in a reference to the strikers' twenty-one demands, said simply, "21 × TAK," meaning "21 TIMES YES." A year later, a ubiquitous poster sums up the national frustration: "STILL, AFTER A FULL YEAR, ONLY 2 × YES AND 19 × NO." The only demands that have in fact been honored, according to this slogan, concern (1) the registration of an independent, self-governing trade union with (2) the right to strike. Most of the government's other concessions, in areas such as health and working conditions, have gone largely unfulfilled.

Some commentators think that in the heat of the moment, in order to end the strike, the government made concessions that, given economic and geopolitical realities, it knew it could never honor and that it secretly hoped it would never have to honor: there was a vague sense that this revolution couldn't possibly last, that no one would be held accountable in the long run. "Even today," a prominent documentary filmmaker told me in Warsaw, "the Party behaves as if this were all just some bad dream from which any moment now it will awaken."

The perversity of the situation lies in the fact that while the country's economy spirals downward, the various leaders who ought to be addressing the crisis are instead expending huge amounts of intellectual, political, psychological, and spiritual energy sparring with each other. The most visible result of the Party congress was not some new economic program but rather the launching of a withering media attack on Solidarity. For several weeks preceding the convening of Solidarity's own First National Congress, in September, the media truce that had been so precariously sustained during the spring was completely suspended, and the airwaves—especially television—bristled with angry, almost hysterical attacks on the union's leadership and its aspirations.

The state media during this period took particular delight in pointing to the Reagan Administration's handling of the air-traffic controllers' strike in America. In essence, the editorial line boiled down to: "See, strikes by government employees are not allowed even in the United States! How dare all of you state-employed workers threaten to strike here?" When I brought this issue up with a union delegate in Warsaw, he said, "The failure of American labor to stand together is a reflection of its inadequacy, not our impertinence. Apart from a few flimsy resolutions and token gestures, the American air controllers' colleagues in labor stood idly by while Reagan gutted the isolated union." He pointed to a badge he was wearing on his chest. "Look, see this badge? What does it tell you? My name and region—not my trade. From this badge, you can't tell if I'm a coal miner, an editor, or an air-traffic controller. We are organized by region, in solidarity—not by trade, in isolation. If American labor had been similarly organized this summer, Reagan would never have been able to emasculate your air-traffic controllers."

As the date of the Solidarity congress approached, labor unrest spread from factories and transportation networks into newsrooms and printing plants: workers belonging to Solidarity refused to publish the increasingly high-strung government tirades. As the economy lay reeling, Solidarity and the government entered into negotiations on access to the media—among other things, on whether Solidarity could have its own columns in the standard newspapers and its own time slots on television, especially during the congress. Solidarity did achieve a few uncensored moments on television just before the opening of the first session, but then the negotiations broke down completely. As one of the first orders of buisness, the eight hundred and ninety-odd delegates to the Solidarity congress voted to ban Polish television cameras from the hall altogether.

Typical of the energy being lavished by both sides on these skirmishes was the Ongoing Incident of the Wall at the Gdansk train station. Along the far wall of the station, parallel with and fronting all the incoming tracks, some of Solidarity's midnight commandos had scrawled in huge, bright white letters, "DON'T BELIEVE WHAT THEY SAY ON TELEVISION—TV IS LYING!" The next day, the rail-yard administrators managed to put together a twenty-five-car empty train, which they parked in front of the offending message, blocking it from everyone's view. That night, the Solidarity people scrawled the same message on the train cars. The next afternoon, as I was passing the station on the way to the congress, I could see several rail-yard officials out on the tracks uncoupling the cars and rearranging the train. "Great," an American reporter sharing the taxi with me said. "Real good use of energy and time."

Olivia Sports Arena, a few miles north of the Gdansk shipyards, is a sleek, modern facility with a soaring roof. For six days beginning on September 5th, and another twelve days beginning on September 26th, it was the site for the two sessions of the First National Congress of Solidarity Delegates. (During the two-week break, delegates returned home to consult with their constituents.) Outside, townspeople milled around at all hours, listening to the deliberations piped through loudspeakers, exchanging hunches, and trading—not selling—Solidarity pins and memorabilia from the various regions.

Reporters from Polish television sulked, trying vainly to snag anyone they could find into talking before their cameras. Dozens of buses from all over Poland were ranged in the arena's large parking lot, festooned with all sorts of art and posters. One popular broadside proclaimed, simply, "SOLIDARNOSC: 10,000,000 SOLID"; another, the congress's official announcement, featured a large photograph of a toddler—a plump little kid in a Solidarity T-shirt launching into his first confident steps. The two posters summed up what was perhaps the most awesome achievement of the congress—the fact that it was taking place at all. Barely a year old, Solidarity not only had acquired a membership of approximately ten million but, through an elaborate, decentralized process, had even managed to include all ten million in the sequence of grass-roots balloting, local caucuses, and regional congresses that finally selected the representatives who were gathering in the hall.

Inside the arena, beneath large, colorful banners, the delegates sat in rows of chairs arranged by region. Only six per cent were women.[13] The average age was thirty-six. Half the delegates were university graduates—a figure that some observers found surprisingly, disquietingly high. Every twentieth delegate belonged to the Polish Communist Party. (Of the Party's three million members, one million belong to Solidarity.)

In tiers of seats angled high above the floor were the journalists, many of them Western and struggling with the appallingly primitive and static-ridden simultaneous-translation headsets. ("I'm sure these things are giving my ears cancer," muttered one British reporter as he jammed the devilish devices deeper into his ears and cocked his neck into the best, if least comfortable, receiving position.) A curious double flow of condescension seemed to develop: the Western reporters smiled expansively at the delegates ("Oh, isn't it cute how they're trying to master this democratic process!"), and the delegates indulged in their own smug estimation of the reporters ("Oh, isn't it cute how they're straining to fathom the unique Polish soul!").

In the front of the auditorium, an elaborate scoreboard—a computer-controlled pattern of lights—was emblazoned almost the entire time with a huge pointillist rendition of a cross. The congress opened with an emotional Solemn Mass, celebrated in the nearby Oliwa Cathedral by Jozef Glemp, the new primate of Poland (heir to Cardinal Wyszynski, who had died early in the summer). No one missed the symbolism: unlike the Communist Party congress in July, this meeting had the imprimatur of all of Polish history.

As if to hammer the point home, Lech Walesa, in his opening address, singled out the observers from the government: "I welcome first of all the representatives of the government. We are independent and self-governing"—the phrase set off an outburst of applause—"but we are active within the state, and as hosts of the present congress we respectfully welcome the arrival of the government delegation." He paused—there was no applause—and then continued, "I am not a diplomat, so I will be frank. Up to the very last minute before the opening of the present congress, a number of actions were being launched and a number of words were being spoken that might have been avoided. We are expected to answer various questions. We shall debate them. But it is also we who are expecting an answer to the basic question. A year ago, we said that we are talking 'like a Pole to a Pole.' Now, twelve months of many conflicts later, we want to know whether we shall continue to talk like that." These remarks—so characteristic of Walesan rhetoric—were at once passionately earnest and dripping with irony. Twelve months earlier, after the exhausting negotiations between the strikers and Mieczyslaw Jagielski, the government's chief negotiator, which concluded the shipyard strike, Walesa had graciously agreed with Jagielski's statement that they had spoken "like a Pole to a Pole." Jagielski had since been purged, wiped out in the balloting at the Party congress in July—presumably for his part in the Gdansk capitulation—and now Walesa was asking the new officials if Solidarity would be able to talk to them "like a Pole to a Pole." There was no question that Solidarity was Polish (after all, just hours earlier they had celebrated Mass with the very embodiment of Polish history)—the only question was whether this government and the Party that controlled it were Polish. The crowd went wild.

It was the last sign of life from the delegates for several days. The congress quickly lapsed into a morass of procedural wrangling, parliamentary maneuvering, and ceremonial greeting. (In one strange moment, the emissary from the West German federation of trade unions, Ervin Kristoffersen, offered the delegates his opinion that "order without freedom cannot last long, but freedom also calls for order." Some of the delegates wondered what business a German emissary had offering Poles advice of any kind.) For hour after hour, the delegates sat, pasty-faced, absorbing the miasma. ("Banning television from the congress was the smartest thing Solidarity could have done," a friend remarked to me. "The coverage so far would have been embarrassingly dull. Instead, we get to watch the spectacle of the TV people, banned from the hall, having to report each night from their pathetic stations outside the auditorium. The look on their faces—it's great!") At one point, one of the delegates met me outside for a smoke. "Boy, this democracy may be worth dying for, but it can kill you with boredom once you've got it," he said. At another point, I asked Jan Litynski if people were getting disappointed at the slow pace of the proceedings. "Yes," he replied. "People are even getting angry, but the trouble is they're getting angry in different directions." Jan Rulewski, one of the leaders of the Bydgoszcz delegation, and considered by some delegates one of the most hotheaded figures at the convention, was surprisingly understanding. "Keep in mind," he told me, "that we are trying to coördinate the thinking of ten million people here. This is our first meeting. Of course if takes time." One of the townspeople listening to the proceedings over the loudspeakers was even more indulgent. "Hell," he exclaimed, "the Communist Party congress took *seven* days, and they weren't talking about anything! These people are trying to save the nation."

Beneath the deadly dull surface, however, powerful forces were already at work, as would presently become clear. For as the speeches and motions dragged on, the delegates were gradually orienting themselves with regard to the three principal issues that would come to dominate the congress: the problem of democratic process within the union; the question of how hard the union should push the Polish state and the Communist Party in demanding decentralized self-management at the workplace; and—somewhat more amorphous but perhaps most crucial of all—the question of whether the delegates, mindful of the history of Polish rebellion, could overcome a centuries-old tradition of romantic, doomed grand gestures.

The dilemma Solidarity faces concerning internal democratic process is this: its principal claim to legitimacy lies in the democratic contrast it offers to the arbitrary, authoritarian alternative embodied in the Party; Solidarity's principal chance for survival, however, derives precisely from its *solidarity*—the fundamental unity of some ten million workers. Ten million people belong to Solidarity because it is democratic and participatory—but if ten million people (or their eight hundred and ninety-odd representatives in Gdansk) were really to start behaving democratically, if differences over fundamental issues were allowed to lead to the formation of hardened factions, then the union's very existence could come into jeopardy. Conversely, in a situation that requires ten million members to speak as one, there is a perennial danger that an individual spokesman for the ten million may begin speaking on their behalf without their authorization. Authenticity, authority, authorization—these are the crucial but evanescent components of Solidarity's fragile achievement.

Even before the congress convened, Adam Michnik, the KOR activist, in an anniversary essay published in the journal *Niezaleznosc,* marvelled at the paradoxical nature of Solidarity: "a movement . . . that combines cult of the leader with an insistence on democracy verging on pathology, and surprising wisdom with rarely encountered naïveté."

Although his name was seldom mentioned, much of the procedural debate during the first several days of Solidarity's congress could be summarized under the simple rubric: what to do with Lech Walesa. Veterans of populist and radical conventions in the United States and Western Europe could recognize a familiar pattern in the proceedings: humiliate the leadership and then reëlect it.

Walesa is almost the same age as the Communist system he is attempting to transform; he is very much the product of the postwar Polish order. Born in 1943 near Lipno, a farming community about halfway between Warsaw and Gdansk, Walesa never really knew his father, a peasant carpenter; two years after the son's birth, the father died of privations he had suffered in a Nazi prison camp. Lech's mother presently married her late husband's brother, and some years afterward mother and stepfather left for the United States. Lech, for his part, attended technical school, served his mandatory term in the Polish Army (he achieved the rank of corporal), and then joined hundreds of thousands of Polish peasant youths in abandoning rural life for jobs in the newly expanding industrial centers. Walesa became an electrical technician in the Gdansk shipyards. (Many of the eventual leaders of Solidarity, including Andrzej Gwiazda, from Gdansk, and Zbigniew Bujak, the head of the Warsaw region, began as electrical or heating technicians—jobs that allowed them to circulate freely through their plants, to converse with workers at all levels, and, as one of them told me, "to get to know how the place was put together.") Walesa was only twenty-seven in 1970, but he was active in the December events, was elected to the strike committee, and represented strikers at a meeting with Edvard Gierek, the new Party chief, in January, 1971. His activities, like virtually everyone else's, were subdued during the early seventies (partly out of a sense of defeat and partly, perhaps, out of a cautious hope that things might actually improve under Gierek), but by the mid-seventies he was again active. Following a fiery speech in April, 1976, he was sacked from his job at the shipyard, and during the next four years he endured a succession of odd jobs and frequent forty-eight-hour arrests. (The final arrest occurred on July 31, 1980, when he was picked up outside his apartment as his wife was on the verge of entering the labor which would culminate, while Walesa was still in jail, in the birth of their sixth child.) Between 1976 and 1980, Walesa developed close relations with members of KOR and participated in the formation of the minuscule Baltic Free Trade Union, the seed from which Solidarity presently sprang.

Walesa's August 1980 exploits, which began during the strike's first hours, with his scaling of the shipyard's walls to get inside, have already achieved the status of legend in Poland, and his own accounts have become subsumed to the requirements of myth. It is clear that almost from the start Walesa served as a charismatic leader, calm but firm in negotiations, flamboyant and inspirational in public speeches; that he had a particularly fine sense of the mood of the crowd and a conviction that it was necessary for the leadership never to vault too far ahead of that mood; and that his abrupt, ironic personal style utterly captivated both the Poles and the Western press.

And still today, a year later, that charisma persists. As he enters the hall, the delegates seem to stir. Everyone is aware of his presence—where he is, what he is doing, how he is reacting—at all times, no matter what else is going on. Lech Walesa has tremendous authority—or, rather, he has been vested with tremendous authority. When you talk to Poles individually, they will list his shortcomings—he is not very well educated, he is sometimes arrogant, he is perhaps too strongly influenced by the moderates in the Church, his Polish is less than elegant. "But," they will invariably conclude, "we need someone like him—the movement needs the kind of focus he provides."

This sense of authenticity, of legitimacy, of authority, is perhaps the key element in Polish political life today. Some people have it; they can transmit it to others or confirm it in each other. Much of this circulation and recirculation of authenticity takes place across a series of images—photographs that recur on the walls of thousands of Polish homes and factories. There is the cherished image of Cardinal Wyszynski, the old man, the beloved grandfather figure, the embodiment of the persistence of the Polish spirit despite years of foreign domination. Then, there is a photograph you see everywhere: Wyszynski bowing and kissing the hand of his onetime protégé, the former archbishop of Krakow, now suddenly the Pope, John Paul II. In that image you can just see the authority coursing from the one to the other. (An oil painting of that photograph has already joined the baroque succession of images of kings and saints gracing the alcoves at the national shrine in Czestochowa.) Often next to that photograph you will see another: John Paul II greeting Lech Walesa at the Vatican. In this picture, authority flows, clearly, from father to son. "We have a new trinity here in Poland," a taxi-driver in Gdansk told me, half seriously, one afternoon. "John Paul II is our father, Walesa is his son, and the 1970 martyrs are the Holy Spirit."

There are other images as well. For example, in the new documentary *Farmers '81,* which is a chronicle of the negotiations that culminated in the registration of Rural Solidarity, the agricultural union, one can see how the talks were floundering until Walesa personally intervened, leading a delegation from Solidarity headquarters in Gdansk. He hardly says anything—just sits there, puffing his pipe thoughtfully—but things begin to happen. Higher government officials arrive to advance the negotiations, the pace quickens, and then, suddenly, there is agreement. At the victory celebration, Walesa joins his hand high in the air with that of Jan Kulaj, the young leader of Rural Solidarity. Kulaj is huge, a towering, robust figure, and Walesa seems to dangle limply by his side. Even so, it is clear which way the authority is flowing.

And there is another, somewhat more curious instance of the phenomenon in Wajda's *Man of Iron.* In one of the film's most touching scenes, Agnieszka, the onetime film chronicler of the 1970 martyr Birkut, is marrying Birkut's son, Tomczyk, who will go on to become a leader of the 1980 strike. The year is perhaps 1978, the scene a Gdansk church. Within the context of the film's fictive reality, this is the marriage of the New Polish Woman and the New Polish Man. There are only two witnesses, friends from the shipyard and its as yet underground dissident movement: Anna Walentynowicz, the crane-operator heroine whose dismissal was partly responsible for setting off the 1980 strike, and Lech Walesa. Playing themselves: offering flowers and soft teasing. It's a very strange moment—you don't know who is conferring authenticity on whom. But the audiences love it, and there's not a dry eye in the house.

Recently a new image has been added to this rosary

chain of legitimization. Solidarity offices all over the country are selling photographs of Marshal Josef Pilsudski, Poland's leader between the wars. Historians rate Pilsudski an ambiguous figure at best: he was something of a populist, but also something of a Fascist. Poles today celebrate him partly because he headed the nation during much of the only period in recent centuries when Poland can be said to have been truly free and independent, but especially because he headed the Polish nationalist army which triumphantly routed the invading Bolshevik Russian force in August, 1920. The thing you notice about this picture, however, is that with his heavy, dark, droopy mustache, the marshal looks uncannily like Lech Walesa.

"Walesa isn't antidemocratic, he's ademocratic," Jan Litynski, the KOR activist, tells me one afternoon. The situation in which Walesa and the rest of the Solidarity leadership have had to work during the past year has often rendered consideration of some of the finer points of democratic process something of a luxury. Crises arise and they have to be addressed immediately. Afterward, however, there is often a residue of resentment at how decisions were reached. The resentment is particularly pronounced among those who feel that the concessions were too large, the compromises too harsh. Thus, it is usually the union's more radical and adventuresome elements who, when objecting to the content of decisions, prefer to phrase their objections in terms of the method by which the decisions were reached. There's no particular reason to believe that the majority of the union's members didn't agree with a particular compromise, but since they weren't consulted anyway, it's fairly easy to cast the concessions as a failure of democratic process.

The debate drags on. Leszek Szaruga, an intellectual who works for the Solidarity press office, walks outside for a breather and speaks of the union's need to defer certain aspects of democratic process for the time being.

"The government's attack on us is highly centralized and coördinated," he explains. "We need a leadership with the authority to respond in kind. We have to be able to counter their propaganda attacks and to strategize our own campaigns, and we can't be expected to go back to the membership for consultations every time."

A few minutes later, Litynski comments, "It's very hard. We are trying to find an authentic way of conducting internal politics—one that will allow us to consider positions and alternatives without factionalizing into categories like 'radicals' and 'moderates,' which is precisely what the Party would like us to do."

One morning, things get out of hand. A proposal is made to separate the functions of the regional leader from those of the regional delegate to the national coördinating committee, which Walesa heads. According to the proposal, no one will be allowed to hold both posts simultaneously. In effect, Walesa's committee would be reduced to a discussion club, since all power would rest with the regional heads, none of whom would be on the committee. The debate takes the form of "dictatorship versus democracy"; the votes are cast, they are being tallied, the proposal seems on the verge of victory, when suddenly Walesa bounds furiously up to the rostrum. Any semblance of parliamentary procedure evaporates. Walesa is, of course, allowed to speak. He orders a ten-minute recess, and when the delegates return, he tells them that he's tired of this nonsense, the country is in the grip of a terrible economic crisis, that that's what the nation is waiting for this congress to confront, and if it's not willing to do so then he's going to have to do things himself, dictator or no. He finishes by demanding that the vote be taken over again. It is, and he wins.

But the cost is high. Walesa's stature is lessened by the whole episode. He has lost—he has spent—some of his authority. Karol Modzelewski, one of Solidarity's leading theorists, remarks later in the afternoon, "It was not a very fortunate thing for the political education and evolution of the union as a whole. The debate was phrased all wrong—between dictatorship and democracy—when it should have been seen as a choice between two ways of doing things, each with certain advantages and certain disadvantages." The union moves on to other business, but the dilemmas concerning authority and internal democratic process remain.

Each morning, as the buses converge on the arena from the various schools and halls and church basements where the representatives are spending their nights, they pass the ever-lengthening lines in front of the ever-emptying shops. It isn't as if the delegates need the reminder, but there it is anyway: Poland's economic situation is dire.

Poland's economy has become entangled in a series of double binds. The situation in Silesia, the coal-rich region to the south, is typical. Coal production is perhaps the most crucial element in Poland's national economy. Coal does more than provide for the bulk of Poland's own energy requirements—when production is going well, it also becomes one of the country's major exports and a principal source of hard currency. In 1979, coal production reached an all-time high of two hundred and four million tons, but production has since fallen by almost twenty per cent, and the grim anticipation for 1981 is a mere hundred and sixty-eight million tons. In 1979, Poland was able to export forty million tons, yielding a hard-currency profit of three billion dollars. In 1981, Poland will be lucky to export ten million tons. The pattern recurs in other industries. For lack of hard currency, Poland cannot buy the spare parts to repair its failing machinery or the raw materials to supply its manufacturing sector, and productivity declines further.

In the coal region, as elsewhere, one of the major causes of the drop in productivity is that, thanks to the success of their movement, the workers—the miners—

now get Saturdays off. The government has tried to entice the miners back to work on Saturdays with offers of triple pay, but they tend to ignore the offer, since the money is worthless and there's nothing to buy in the shops anyway. Thus, the vicious circle: there's nothing to buy because, for lack of hard currency, the state can import neither consumer goods and food nor the spare parts and equipment that could help Poland to produce its own; the only way to generate the hard currency is to get the workers to work harder, but they have no incentive to work harder, because there's nothing they could buy with any extra money they might earn. Solidarity spokespeople point to that vicious circle, and to the atrocious record of administrative mismanagement that characterized the Gierek years, in offering their own solution to the economic crisis: *samorzad,* or worker self-management. It is their answer to almost every economic question you ask. Sometimes it's an answer that provokes more questions than it resolves.

Back in August, 1980, Solidarity was reluctant to press the issue of *samorzad,* partly because of a prior history of disappointments. In 1956 and 1970, the authorities had responded to crises by drafting supposed reforms, instituting "worker self-management" arrangements of various kinds, but in the long run nothing had changed: beneath the wordplay, power remained vested in the Party bureaucrats. Solidarity was also reluctant to take on the management of the economy that was clearly in a lot of trouble, paticularly within the framework of the kind of partial participation the government seemed to be offering: not enough authority to make the necessary reforms but just enough so that Solidarity could end up catching most of the blame for the coming collapse. Finally, Solidarity still saw itself as a trade union—a vigilant protector of its workers' interests but not the kind of organization that wanted to become a quasi-authority in its own right. Solidarity preferred to respond to the government's initiatives.

As time passed, however, the economic situation worsened, and the Party and the government seemed paralyzed. "Vigilance alone was not enough," Solidarity decided, according to an official in its press office. "What were we to be vigilant about if the government rendered no decisions?" By early spring of 1981, many Solidarity chapters were beginning to frame proposals for worker self-management. These proposals invariably grew out of a consistent double critique of the current arrangement. Solidarity's theorists argued that one principal cause of the economic debacle was the overcentralized character of state planning: the system was top-heavy, inflexible, barely responsive. It wasn't difficult to come up with a parade of ludicrous examples to prove that point. But Solidarity also attacked the way in which the upper- and middle-level bureaucratic slots were filled; Solidarity began to confront *nomenklatura.*

Nomenklatura is an elaborate system whereby the Communist Party exercises the right to appoint the top hundred thousand bureaucrats and administrators in Poland. Whatever the internal structure of an organization, the Party selects, usually from within its own ranks, the heads of all the important sectors. There's a list—*nomenklatura*—which is continually being refined, and if a person is not on that list he's not eligible for a given administrative post. Whatever can be said about the idealistic intentions with which this system was originally devised (a vanguard Party's way of coordinating the tremendously complex and interconnected aspects of a ravaged country's postwar reconstruction, for example), *nomenklatura* has for the most part degenerated into a lunatic collage of incompetence, privilege pandering, and outright corruption. "The administrative overseer of our unit," a filmmaker tells me, "got the job because, having failed as a diplomat, he was brought back to Warsaw and he requested job placement within walking distance of his home. Our studio happens to be three blocks away. I don't think he'd ever seen a film."

"Of course, *nomenklatura* has produced some good managers," a delegate to the convention conceded to me one day, "but they are the exception, and in this crisis, good management must become the rule."

Solidarity's insistence on worker self-management is, therefore, a double demand, both for decentralization of decision-making and for greater worker participation in the making of those decisions.

There are various schemes for *samorzad,* but the basic idea goes something like this: the enterprise (factory, publishing house, airline, or whatever) would be the communal property of the workers who run it. (Today, it belongs to the state, which, in turn, supposedly—but only supposedly—belongs to the workers.) The workers would elect a representative council, subject to continuing review and to recall, and the council would appoint a manager, who would be responsible to the council alone. The state would exercise its influence through economic instruments (taxes, duties, investment credits, etc.) or normative laws (regulations, pollution standards, etc.), but otherwise it would stay out and allow the free play of the market to rationalize the economy. Workers' councils at various large enterprises—some factories have already elected such councils, which have been exerting varying degrees of influence, though nothing near what they eventually hope to achieve— would form interconnecting bodies. Already, an entity called Network joins representatives from Solidarity branches at the Gdansk shipyards, the Katowice coal mines, the Ursus truck plant near Warsaw, the steel mills outside Krakow, and several other large enterprises in a kind of self-management study group.

Eventually, according to several theorists, each factory might contain two parallel organizations—a trade union and a workers' council. Many Solidarity officials have noted that the union cannot be expected to represent all its members as workers and at the same time develop managerial and marketing strategies that might prove detrimental to individual subgroups of its membership. Earlier this year, Zbigniew Bujak, the Solidarity leader for the Warsaw region, who has all along been one of the more farsighted strategists in this area, theorized that a workers' council might earmark a certain share of the profits for, say, capital investment and expansion, while the trade union might insist that the money instead go into safety improvements and workers' pensions. Negotiations would then occur between the council and the union.

It is difficult to imagine how such a theory would work in practice, and Western reporters tend to besiege Solidarity's theorists with their misgivings. How can the same body of workers act as both management and labor in any given negotiation? What of the lack of managerial experience and skills on the part of workers who are suddenly asked to map out—or, at least, decide on—strategies of investment, planning, marketing, and so forth? What of the need for central planning—for a centralized coördination of response to what is, after all, a nationwide crisis? Isn't it conceivable that, for example, profits from coal should go into agriculture? Then how is that transfer to be effected in a decentralized system of self-managing units? What if a shipyard democratically chose to build a certain kind of tanker, and the workers at the relevant steel mill simultaneously decided that they no longer wanted to make the required kind of steel? What if the workers in a shipyard decided they didn't want to fill an order from, say, the Soviet Union, because they could get more hard currency from the West? (Is the Soviet response going to be decentralized?) Is it fair to expect steelworkers at a thirty-year-old plant to compete with those at a plant that has just been opened, as if the two were setting out on an equal footing? And isn't Solidarity's own experience of democratic process—the convoluted movement and the agonizingly slow pace of the process—cause for concern when Solidarity is advocating its transposition into the economic realm, where decisions have to be made within the context of a world market that is constantly changing at the speed of a computer printout?

Unfortunately, the answers one gets to such questions are usually fairly glib. Generally, they fall into three categories: (1) "You can't understand, because you're not Polish. We Poles have a special history—of nationalism (even though it's been thwarted) and socialism (even though it's become deformed)—that has prepared us for the task of transcending such problems." (2) "What do you expect? We're only one year old. It takes time to develop all those details. You're asking way too much of us." (3) "That's not our problem—that's the government's problem."

My favorite conversation along these lines occurred with Stanislaw Fudakowski, an industrial psychologist and a member of the Gdansk delegation to the congress. It was late in the day, and the condescension, I'm afraid, was flowing hot and heavy in both directions. "Look," he finally said. "You're American, so perhaps these questions make sense to you, but they have little relevance to us. One of the main things to understand is that the strategy of insisting on self-management allows us to confront the centralized power of the state without ever having to confront it directly. Little by little, authority will be transferred to the local level, until in the end the state will have lost most of its power."

"Fine," I said. "But Poland owes the Western banks and governments, for example, around twenty-five billion dollars. Who's going to be responsible for paying that debt?"

"That," he smiled, "is the government's problem."

"Of course there are contradictions," the filmmaker

Andrzej Chodakowski sighed one afternoon after I paraded my cavalcade of misgivings. "The situation is so tremendously botched up at this point—the status quo itself is so loaded with contradictions—that any response will also have certain contradictions. Basically, we are struggling to find some way of introducing competition without private ownership, in such a way that the losers in the competition will still be somehow protected. It's not easy—there are no models. But, seriously, it can't get any worse than what we've got. Anything would be an improvement over *nomenklatura.*"

"Self-management may not solve everything," Karol Modzelewski explained to a group of reporters outside the hall. "But we've got to find some way of *institutionalizing* the integration of the workers' wishes into the decision-making process, without always having to have recourse to strikes, with the tremendous tension and danger they arouse."

"Self-management may not solve everything," Tadeusz Mazowiecki, the editor of Solidarity's national weekly paper, told another group of reporters, a few feet away. "But we expect it to increase worker interest and therefore productivity. If workers are working for themselves, they will be willing to make the sacrifices the situation demands. They won't do it for worthless pay increases or if they feel that their labor only enriches their bosses, but they may do it for themselves."

Sitting in the gallery, watching the debate, I was reminded of something that Ludwig Wittgenstein once wrote: "Philosophy unties knots in our thinking; hence its results must be simple; but philosophizing has to be as complicated as the knots it unties." The same could be said of the possibilities for political renewal in Poland today.

Actually, many of the contradictions that Western reporters point to in Solidarity's proposals are more apparent than real. When you really press the issue, it turns out that the debate isn't finally about ongoing democratic process in the workplace. Solidarity's membership by and large understands the need for strong and decisive management at the factory level. What it is trying to confront is the way that that management is chosen, the system of *nomenklatura*. It is trying to save the Polish economy by replacing incompetent, corrupt, and aloof administrators with competent, honest, and responsive ones, and by making them responsible to the workers. The frightening thing, as the first session nears its climax, is that while Solidarity seems willing to go to the wall on this point, it is the one issue on which the Polish Communist Party seems unwilling to budge. The Party can change faces at the top so easily precisely because its true control of the nation lies in its hold on the middle bureaucracy. A compromise had seemed possible back in March—there were promising signs from both sides—but then the first Bydgoszcz crisis erupted: three Solidarity members (Jan Rulewski was one of them) were savagely beaten by local police officers. Some people think that this incident was orchestrated by frightened middle-level bureaucrats intent on polarizing the situation and scuttling any compromise. That, at any rate, was the outcome. During the summer, the government drafted its own new law on worker self-management—a patently obvious attempt at coöptation that seemed even more transparent than the 1956 and 1970 reformist charades—which it began quickly moving through the Party-controlled national parliament. Solidarity's Network countered with its own "Draft of a Bill on Social Enterprises." On September 8th, as the parliament's vote neared, the Solidarity congress voted an ultimatum. The parliament had three options: (1) scuttle the government version and enact Solidarity's plan; (2) hold a national referendum and let the people decide between the two plans; or (3) Solidarity itself would hold the referendum. There was little doubt about how the people would vote in such a referendum. The implication was that if the government failed to honor its results, Solidarity might have recourse to a general strike.

"This is it," one heard over and over in the halls outside the auditorium. "We are nearing confrontation." A new mood was emerging at the congress: a combination of elation and gloom, a double sense of dynamic vitality and impending disaster.

One afternoon, John Darnton and I were catching a bite outside the hall, and he commented, "This congress is just like the New York City Council, which I used to cover. Things seem to be going along at a crawl, but you can't turn your back on them for a minute—they're likely to do just about anything while you're not looking."

A few days later, near the conclusion of the first session of the congress, I got a chance to see what he meant. I was out by the headset table, trying to contrive a combination of earplugs, batteries, and receivers that might in fact deliver something other than inchoate electricity to my sorry ears, when a huge ovation burst out from inside the hall. Jamming the plugs back into my tender head, I raced back to the bleachers and sought out the group of reporters with whom I'd taken to sitting. Their faces were incredulous, unbelieving. "What on earth are they doing that for?" one of them muttered. "They need this headache?" "Tell you one thing," put in another, "they're sure going out with a bang."

Solidarity had just voted to send a letter of greeting "to the working people of Albania, Bulgaria, Czechoslovakia, the German Democratic Republic, Rumania, Hungary, and all the nations of the Soviet Union." The letter read, in part, "We assure you that despite the lies spread all over your countries, we are an authentic organization of ten million workers. . . . We support those of you who have embarked upon the difficult road of struggle for the free trade-union movement. We believe that it shall not be long before our representatives meet yours to exchange experiences."

The next morning, *Trybuna Ludu,* the Polish Communist Party paper, published the entire text of the letter in the course of attacking it, paragraph by paragraph. For the first time in a long while, the paper sold out almost immediately.

Now, as the first session of the congress rushed toward adjournment for its two-week break, the predictable fire storm erupted. In Moscow, the reaction was furious. On the evening news, workers at the Zil truck plant outside Moscow were shown approving a reply to Solidarity's insolent note. As the Manchester *Guardian* reported the next day, the Zil letter "told the Poles that their country owed its existence to the Soviet Union, and that they should get back to work rather than follow the 'demagogues' of Solidarity." Throughout Eastern Europe—even in Hungary, which up to that point had been relatively tolerant—government spokespeople and journalists joined in the condemnation. The Polish Party's Politburo held an emergency meeting and within a few days released its most fiercely worded attack yet on anti-socialist elements and tendencies in Solidarity. A few days after that, it became clear that the Polish Politburo was acting in response to a harrowing ultimatum it had received from its Soviet counterpart. For the first time, it appeared—and various rumors heightened the sense of impending calamity—that the Soviet Union had threatened crippling cutbacks in its delivery of vital resources, including oil, if the Polish Party did not quickly reassert its authority. (Poland gets ninety-five per cent of its oil from the Soviet Union.)

This sudden flareup of tension highlighted the misperceptions prevalent on all sides. On the one hand, Soviet commentators tend to blame Solidarity for Poland's current economic crisis: they blame the union for disastrous declines in productivity as a result of time wasted in anarchistic politicking and pointless strikes. Jan Litynski of KOR counters that the country was headed for an economic catastrophe in any case, owing to mismanagement and the disastrous foreign debt. "As the food lines lengthen, as shortages spread, Solidarity is the only thing keeping this country from ripping itself apart, from descending into wholesale food riots and anarchy," Litynski argues. "People are still channelling their anger into constructive criticism, but only because such a channel exists."

On the other hand, many Solidarity members put the blame for the economic crisis entirely on the Soviet Union. Each time a train leaves Poland heading east, freighted with coal or sulfur or grain, Poles begrudge what they perceive to be their colonial fate, their status as continuing victims of the Soviet leech. "But that's one perception they've got all wrong," insists the otherwise sympathetic Daniel Singer. "Sure, the Poles send the Russians various quantities of goods, but they are receiving much more than they're giving." (Poland gets ninety-five per cent of its natural gas and ninety per cent of its iron ore from the Soviet Union.) "The Russians have been willing to go along with the situation," Singer continues, "for fear of the consequences of the complete collapse that might otherwise take place. But the Russian patience may not last forever. Indeed, the current crisis is occurring because the Russians are threatening to cut back their oil shipments not to some arbitrary level but, rather, to the precise amount that the Poles can pay for, in cash or barter—which is to say virtually nothing. That, of course, would be a disaster."

In any event, the question remains: Why has Solidarity done it? Why, after carefully avoiding provocations of any kind—especially cheap ones, especially anti-Soviet ones—has the union suddenly thrown just

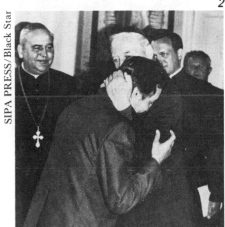

For the Poles, the continuity of legitimacy and authenticity often takes place across a series of images—photos framed in homes or scenes glimpsed in films. Thus, for example, in Figure 1 we see the beloved Polish archbishop Stefan Wyszynski bowing before his onetime protégé, Karol Wojtyla, who has just become Pope. In Figure 2, Wyszynski in turn greets Lech Walesa, as does John Paul himself in Figure 3. In both cases, they endow the union leader with some of their authority. Walesa, in turn, endows Andrzej Wajda's film Man of Iron with Solidarity's imprimatur when he and Anna Walentynowicz appear in a scene (Fig. 4) portraying the marriage of the film's fictional protagonists, Tomczyk (Jerzy Radziwilowicz) and Agnieszka (Krystyna Janda). See discussion on pages 52 and 97.

UPI

SIPA PRESS/Black Star

SYGMA

United Artists Classics

Edvard Gierek is applauded at the Eighth Congress of the Polish Communist Party —February 1980.

Communist Party hard-liner Stefan Olszowski, General Wojciech Jaruzelski, and party First Secretary Stanislaw Kania in September 1981, on the eve of Kania's resignation and replacement by Jaruzelski

Czeslaw Milosz, Nobel Prize-winning poet

Issac Bashevis Singer, Nobel Prize-winning novelist

Andrzej Wajda, film director

Warsaw citizens in line for food, September 1981

September 1981: The first national congress of Solidarity delegates convenes in Gdansk with over 850 freely elected representatives from throughout Poland.

Stanislaw Bury, Gdansk shipyard branch leader, with Walesa at Solidarity Congress.

Lech Walesa (note the ever-present pin portraying Our Lady of Czestochowa) confers with Jan Rulewski, a leading Solidarity firebrand from Bydgoszcz.

Veteran Gdansk Solidarity activists Andrzej Gwiazda and Bogdan Lis. (Gwiazda and Rulewski will challenge Walesa for the chairmanship of the union. Lis, incidentally, is only twenty-nine years old.)

KOR *activist Adam Michnik*

KOR *activist Jacek Kuron*

Pełnometrażowy film dokumentalny   o strajku w STOCZNI GDAŃSKIEJ

ROBOTNICY '80

Realizacja: Andrzej Chodakowski
Andrzej Zajączkowski
Zdjęcia: Michał Bukojemski
Jacek Petrycki

A-2 O-13 50 700 egz.

Prod: WFD. WARSZA

I KRAJOWY GDAŃSK '81
ZJAZD DELEGATÓW
NSZZ·SOLIDARNOŚĆ·

PIERWSZY EFEKT
IX ZJAZDU PZPR

OBCIĘCIE RACJI ŻYWNOŚCIOWYCH!

*As Poland entered its second autumn since the advent of Solidarity, the political situation was becoming increasingly precipitous. With Solidarity and the party continually deadlocked, food supplies were dwindling, lines lengthening and spirits flagging. The extreme variations in mood could be seen in Solidarity's ongoing graphic production. Thus, for example, one poster commonly visible in late summer announced Solidarity's upcoming National Congress of Delegates in Gdansk by portraying a chubby, confident baby in a Solidarity T-shirt (and red-and-white trunks) taking his first confident steps: Solidarity at one year old. But, at the same time, walls were plastered with a more primitive, harrowing image, a skull with crossed fork and knife and the legend—*THE FIRST EFFECT OF THE NINTH COMMUNIST PARTY CONGRESS *(just concluded in July):* LOWER FOOD RATIONS.

Poland's graphic artists could see the recent political renewal coming a mile away. Witness the 1979 poster for Janusz Kijow's film **Kung Fu** (above) which dealt with bureaucratic corruption. Similarly powerful was the 1980 poster for **Robotnicy '80** (Workers '80), the remarkable documentary dealing with the August strike negotiations in Gdansk. Anemic by comparison were the contemporaneous offerings of American political artists. In the poster at right for the AFL-CIO's September 19, 1981, "Solidarity Day" demonstrations, note the absence of flags or other emblems of American patriotism (the wording on the poster is in green). When Solidarity offered its May Day 1980 poster, the Polish **masses** were their flag—red on white.

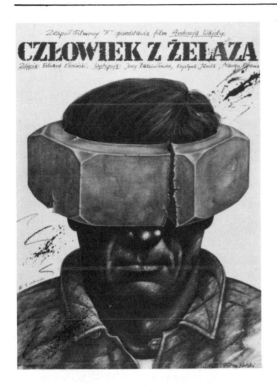

Similarly, posters advertising recent Polish films deployed virtually identical imagery to opposite effect. In one promoting Andrzej Wajda's Man of Iron, the protagonist's vibrant energy seemed focussed on a moment of impending liberation. In another, on behalf of Agnieszka Holland's Fever, all that energy seemed on the verge of blowing itself apart. Vaguely similar imagery, in turn, was displayed in a Solidarity poster advocating member participation in the round of elections leading toward the Gdansk convention: This poster merely insisted "YOU decide," but bold arrows converged on the "YOU," framing it, emphasizing it, and nearly crushing it.

UPI

NBC

During the night of December 12–13, the Polish military under the command of General Jaruzelski accomplished a brilliantly executed lightning coup, bringing Solidarity's sixteen-month experiment with democratic socialism to an abrupt halt. As John Darnton reported in a letter smuggled out to The New York Times *a few days later, "Fear can come back as quickly as a door slamming." Most of Solidarity's national leadership were herded into detention centers following their meeting the previous day in Gdansk; Lech Walesa, himself, was seen shrugging sadly at the conclusion of that meeting, and then not seen again for some time. Where openness and hope had reigned just a few days earlier, such as at Warsaw's National Academy of Sciences portrayed below, there now stretched only the long, dark shadow of a military regime—authority without legitimacy.*

UPI

about the biggest, most gratuitous Soviet-baiting provocation one could imagine?

"Was this," as Daniel Singer wondered by telephone from Paris, "some aberration, or is it rather the first sign of some budding death wish?"

As the days passed—I'd returned to Warsaw—and the prospects indeed seemed to be turning more and more deadly, I couldn't get the question out of my head: Why had they done it?

I remembered an interlude a few days before the resolution to send the letter to the Eastern European countries was passed. The delegates were debating the general economic crisis that day when they suddenly adjourned for an exceptionally long lunch break. The reason, it turned out, was that several delegations needed time to pile into their buses and take the half-hour drive out to Westerplatte, on the narrow spit of land at the head of the Gdansk harbor where, forty-two years earlier, an overwhelmingly outnumbered group of Polish soldiers had held off an invading Nazi landing force for a few days at the outset of the Second World War. The cratered bunker has been left untouched ever since, as a memorial to the fierce but futile defense of the peninsula. An empty tank stands at the entrance to the memorial park in commemoration, and recently Solidarity had erected a simple cross by its side. The delegates were shuttling over to lay a wreath at the foot of the cross.

The country's economy is in shambles, I remember thinking as my taxi dogged the outbound buses. The congress is supposed to be deliberating the issue, and instead here we go on yet another memorial excursion to grieve over yet another martyrdom that happened some forty-odd years ago.

I was sharing the taxi with Henry Feiwel, an American textile wholesaler who was in Poland pricing fabric and had decided to pay a day's visit to the congress.

(Feiwel, a Viennese Jew, had himself narrowly escaped the Holocaust.) As we drove out, the taxi-driver was telling us how we had to understand Polish history, the way the Polish nation had struggled, and so forth.

"This country is obsessed with that sense of history," Feiwel said as we left the taxi and approached the memorial ceremony. "With 1939 and 1944 and 1956 and 1970. They're always telling you how you have to understand their history. But the thing that you have to understand—that *they* have to understand—is the world today, a world in which things move so much faster than they ever have before. In a world like that, in a business climate like that, you don't have time to dwell on things that happened fifty years ago, ten years ago. They shouldn't even spend so much time dwelling on August, 1980. The world is passing them by."

A few days later, I mentioned Feiwel's comment to a Warsaw psychologist.

"I understand what he is saying," the psychologist told me, "but you have to understand that when we speak of 1939, for example, we are not just talking about the past, we are talking about an attitude toward the future. Take that Westerplatte ceremony. At the very moment the delegates were laying those wreaths by the cross, less than a hundred kilometres out at sea the Soviets were holding naval maneuvers, trying to frighten the congress into taking a softer line. On some evenings, I'm told, you could see their battleships from the shore. That ceremony concerned things that happened more than forty years ago, but it was also about what could happen tomorrow. That's what you have to understand about the Eastern European resolution. You see, we Poles live on two parallel time tracks—especially these days. One is rational: If we do this, they will do that, and then we can do such-and-such. But the other is metahistorical. It springs from a long history of defeat and desolation. And it has to do with a sense that a sort of victory can be sprung from defeat. You see, we are always preparing for the worst. There is a conviction that we should behave in such a way that if worst comes to worst, at least our children will have the knowledge that we were a glimmer, that for a brief moment we lit a spark of hope. They will have that knowledge as they sit in their prison cells."

He continued, "We're doomed. Geography dooms us. If Poles had behaved rationally in the past, the Polish nation would not exist today. We would have been absorbed into the Ukraine and Germany; our language, our culture would have long ago disappeared. Poland survives *because* Poles are irrational. It would probably take a tremendous amount of vodka to get them to admit it, but I think that deep down most people have a sense that disaster may well come. That's why the Eastern European resolution was so vital. If disaster comes, at least they'll have something bright and burning to look back to, and therefore to look forward to." (This psychologist, incidentally, was Jewish—one of the group of young Jewish Poles I had met on my May visit. As I listened to him, his every phrase seemed equally charged with Jewish significance.)

The Grand Prize winner at this year's Gdansk Film Festival was *Goraczka (Fever),* Agnieszka Holland's extraordinary portrayal of the tragic fate of a group of Polish-nationalist terrorists during the stillborn 1905 rebellion against the Russian occupying authorities. The tale, replete with police spies, corrupt Polish collaborators, and valiant young patriots, ends almost farcically: everything is botched. Surprisingly, the film was made before August, 1980. The filming was allowed because the nationalists were also socialists, and the Russians were, after all, representatives of the czar. But everybody in the audience knew what the film was really about.

Or another example of the pervasive double entendre which is Polish history: When Poles include 1944 in their rosary of dates, they're not referring to their "liberation" by the Soviet army. It only seems that way. One of Solidarity's newest posters features the date 1944 and a modernist rendition of the heroic wall graffiti,

P for Poland, with an anchor, a longtime token of Polish Catholic nationalism (most recently revived in the Gdansk 1970 memorial). But also PW—*"Polska Walczaca,"* "Poland is still fighting!"—the motto of the Polish Home Army, the *Armia Krajowa,* which led the indigenous resistance to Hitler's occupation. , the symbol of the Warsaw Uprising, the valiant, futile battle waged by Warsaw's home resistance starting August 1, 1944, and then continuing for sixty-three days—while the Soviet army (or so the Poles insist) stalled in its advance, waiting for the Nazis to clean out the nationalists for them.

Or yet another example: In cemeteries throughout Poland, you are likely to happen upon individual plaques almost buried under flowers and student badges. Spread apart the wilting blossoms and you will find the date 1940 and the place of death: Katyn. Several thousand Polish officers were killed in three places that have come to be known collectively as Katyn—a village in western Russia. Officially, according to Soviet and Polish state versions, the massacre took place in 1941, as Hitler's armies barrelled toward Moscow, and the victims were martyrs to Nazism. But most Poles know better: they'll tell you that the massacres took place in 1940, when Soviet forces occupied eastern Poland in the aftermath of the Hitler-Stalin non-aggression pact.

There's no official memorial to Katyn, but every year, on All Saints' Day (November 1st), a particular corner of the huge Powazki Cemetery in Warsaw seems to overflow with a spontaneous laying of wreaths and flowers. Earlier this year (on August 1st, the thirty-sixth anniversary of the launching of the Warsaw Uprising), the local Solidarity chapter erected a simple wooden cross at the site, with the date 1940. It was removed within a single night by the police, but Solidarity is now going ahead with plans for a permanent Katyn memorial at the site. The government is trying to head off the project with a fancy memorial of its own: "Katyn 1941." But Solidarity is not likely to stand for the substitute, and sometime in the months ahead the issue may boil over into an extraordinary crisis.

In Poland today, commemoration is rehearsal. A Pole who lays a wreath in honor of a long-past martyrdom reconfirms the knowledge in his blood that if martyrdom should ever be required of him, future generations of Poles will likewise honor his sacrifice. There are no empty gestures.

"Confrontation." "Confrontation." During the week after the Eastern European resolution, it's the word on everybody's lips. A taxi-driver in Warsaw tells me about the closet in his friend's eighth-floor apartment stocked with dozens of bottles of benzine to be hurled at oncoming tanks—an archetypically Polish romantic gesture. The government issues statement after statement, each more shrill than the one before. A poll appearing in a Warsaw journal this week (the Poles love taking and analyzing polls) reveals that fully forty per cent of those interviewed expect a bloody resolution to the crisis sometime in the near future. Everybody is jumpy: I see people in the middle of the street, in the middle of their day, suddenly break down crying. Many suspect that the government may try to cancel the second session of the congress. Bogdan Lis, Solidarity's deputy chairman, promises in an interview that the second session will take place no matter what— inside the Gdansk shipyards, if necessary, under the protection of the workers. In bars, people talk openly about Solidarity's "welcoming committee" and its plans in case of an invasion or a military takeover—how people are to avoid fighting in the street but instead report to factories; Polish workers will command the seats of industry, and the Russians will not dare fire on factories so important to their own economy.

Is this all presentiment of disaster, one wonders, or simply sentiment? Premonition, or predisposition?

There are medical studies that suggest that some New York City executives have become addicted to the adrenaline rushes that their high-pressure jobs provoke. They come physically to require the high risks their jobs entail. Similarly, perhaps, Poles sometimes seem addicted to the poignancy that their history has engendered in them. Repetition compulsion: they crave another fix.

The Eastern European resolution, at any rate, and the crisis it provokes provide some utterly poignant moments, moments just asking to be memorialized.

But there is something else going on here, this first week after the first session. For thirteen months, the valiant, romantic, quixotic streak in the Polish character—the tendency toward martyrdom—has been held remarkably in check. Why is it breaking out now? The answer, I think, is that the Poles are tired. Fear, frustration, and fatigue are setting in: the lines, the shortages, the anxieties about the coming winter. "It's terrible to live like this, the way *they* are making us live," my taxi-driver in Gdansk tells me. "They're starving us. They don't give us the freedom we need to save ourselves. Look what they're turning us into. Look at these lines. I'd rather fight them in battle than let them defeat us like this."

In May, people asked themselves whether they should expect a Russian invasion, and it was clear that the overwhelming majority of the Poles did not. In September, the question seems to have changed into whether one ought to *hope* for a Russian invasion, and a surprising number of Poles do.[14]

There is an early poem by the Greek modern poet C. P. Cavafy entitled "Waiting for the Barbarians." He describes an antique public square, the citizens huddled, the senate suspended, the emperor and his praetors decked out in their finest robes—everyone tense and expectant, waiting for the barbarians. Evening comes, and suddenly the crowd breaks up, overcome with sorrow and confusion: messengers have arrived from the farthest borders, and there is no sign at all of the barbarians. "And now what shall become of us without any barbarians?" the poet concludes. "Those people were a kind of solution."

Once again, the barbarian demurs. And suddenly the fever breaks. On September 22nd, with a few days to go before the opening of the second half of Solidarity's congress, the union's leaders and the government reach a tentative compromise on the crucial question of worker self-management. In a hastily called meeting of the union presidium—only four of the ten members are present—Walesa wins approval in a three-to-one vote. (Jan Rulewski, of Bydgoszcz, dissents.) The national parliament quickly passes the law, fighting back some attempts by Party hard-liners to gut its compromise provisions. If nothing else, the sense of imminent doom loses some imminence. Nevertheless, there are serious questions about the compromise, in which the Party basically preserves the right to appoint managers in certain strategic industries, and both the union and the Party will nominate managers in other industries, each side reserving a veto power, with deadlocks to be decided by an overseeing court. (The system will not go into effect until January 1st.) Many regional leaders in Solidarity think that the union cut much too soft a deal, and cut it too quickly—that the leadership was stampeded into an inadequate response by the state's (and the Soviet Union's) brilliantly orchestrated crisis. According to an alternative reading, Solidarity has only itself to blame for the scale of the crisis that its Eastern European resolution provoked. At any rate, as the second phase of the congress opens, there is no immediate guarantee that the delegates will ratify the scheme. And, indeed, once the congress reconvenes, on September 26th, the focus quickly shifts from the content of the compromise to the way it was achieved. What happened to democratic process? What about the congress's ultimatum to the parliament, with its call for a national referendum? What right does a small group of "experts" negotiating with a small group of government and Party representatives have to subvert the will of the entire congress? Why couldn't the leadership have waited at least until the congress reconvened, so that the compromise could have been discussed in full and in the open? And what kind of presidium meeting was that, anyway, with only four members present?

Once again, the weight of the moment falls on Walesa. Almost through the sheer force of his personality, he subdues the congress. He tells the delegates not to blame him for the fact that only four people showed up at that meeting. He was sick, he says, but *he* managed to make it—ask the others where they were. In the end, the congress votes a mild reprimand of its leadership for its flouting of democratic process and, on the same day, fêtes Walesa on the occasion of his thirty-eighth birthday.

But again the cost is high. A few days later, when the congress holds its election for union chairman, Walesa wins on the first ballot, outpolling all three opponents. Still, he garners only fifty-five per cent of the delegate vote, for a position that half a year ago he would most likely have won by acclamation. Walesa and his authority—the authority with which his constituents have endowed him—remain one of the principal defenses against complete disaster. Most people count on it. But each time he gets taken to the wall—by the government, the Party, the Russians, or the union itself—he leaves part of that authority behind at the wall, like a smudge. At some point, there may not be enough to stave off a final confrontation. "This would be a fascinating experiment," the filmmaker Andrzej Chodakowski tells me outside the hall, "if we weren't its subjects."

On the question of worker self-management, the congress itself agrees to a compromise: the delegates, while not rejecting the parliament's law outright, still call on their leadership to hold referenda in the factories on certain sections of the law. Just what, exactly, will be done as a result of these referenda remains unclear. In a way, it doesn't matter—these issues are far from settled in any case. As the economic crisis persists, the question of management will continue to fester.

"A partnership being born in terrible pain" is how Tadeusz Mazowiecki once described the relationship between Solidarity and the ruling powers. Karol Modzelewski has put it another way: "We advance across a series of compromises, each of which is unsatisfactory: but the alternative would be disaster." [15]

My last few days in Poland, I took to asking people what they thought might happen over the next several months. Many were of course worried about the coming winter ("This may be the snowflake that breaks the giant's back"), about the possibilities of food riots or transportation breakdowns or old people freezing to death in their homes.

One health worker speculated that the time of greatest danger would come in early spring. "People will survive the winter, but early spring is when people will be at their weakest. It will become warm and wet and muddy, and our supply of soap may have given out completely by then, so people won't be washing—in other words, a perfect breeding ground for bacteria and the outbreak of epidemics. And let me tell you, the health-service system is overstrained already. We will not be able to handle such an outbreak."

Several people speculated about the Polish Army—whether it would obey orders to shoot at Polish workers.

"No. Look at them, they're just young kids serving their two years. They're just like us; they *are* us."

"Yes. You have to have served in the Army to know how they work you and work you on senseless, stupid tasks until you're so tired and disoriented and scared that you'll do anything they say."

"Well, the fact of the matter is that some will and some won't."

One morning, Nina Darnton told me, "On my most pessimistic days—well, not my *most* pessimistic days, which is when I'm trying to imagine an invasion, but on my dark days—I fear that *nothing* will happen, that the situation is completely stalemated, and that Poland will just become an open, festering sore, something like Northern Ireland, forever."

And yet, as Andrzej Chodakowski told me at our last lunch together, "It ought to be possible to imagine a happy resolution for Poland. We have such potential riches—mineral resources, fine agricultural land, a highly developed industrial base, an exceptionally well-educated population (perhaps especially that: the untapped creativity of our people!). Poles are by nature hard workers—we're not like people who've grown up in the sun and would rather be out relaxing on the beach: we're eager to get back to work. It's a question of how to combine all of these elements into an integrated economy, which is really a political question. People will be willing to sacrifice if they believe in the integrity and competence of those who are asking them to sacrifice.

"There's so much slack in Poland right now. America or Japan or Germany would have to put in a tremendous effort to increase productivity by three per cent. If

Poland could ever resolve its political crisis, I bet we could increase our productivity by thirty per cent!"

Perhaps Chodakowski is right, but during the first weeks following the conclusion of Solidarity's congress—I have in the meantime returned to the United States—Poland seems no closer than before to a resolution of its political quandary. Although tensions have subsided from their most recent peak—just before the second session—the atmosphere can hardly be described as calm. The government seems to be testing the unity and resolve of the union through a series of price hikes and provocative detentions (individuals distributing Solidarity fliers, as they have been doing for months, are suddenly being arrested; such arrests occur principally in the middle of the busiest public squares, in the middle of the busiest times of day, as if the authorities were *trying* to spark public confrontations). Wildcat strikes are erupting throughout the country (involving over three hundred thousand workers by mid-October). The Communist Party, under intense pressure from the Soviet Union, ousts Chairman Stanislaw Kania, the nondescript bureaucrat who supplanted Edvard Gierek after August, 1980, and replaces him with General Wojciech Jaruzelski, already the Prime Minister and Defense Minister. (Jaruzelski, generally considered a moderate, derives virtually all of his paradoxical authority from the fact that as Defense Minister during the seventies he refused to order "Polish soldiers to fire on Polish workers"; were he ever to do so, that authority would immediately evaporate. Hence, in a certain sense, he can only retain what limited strength he has by refusing to exercise it.) Walesa, meanwhile, has been trying to deal with his own national commission, a body that was elected at the convention and whose members generally espouse positions considerably more hard-line than his own.

As the month of October progresses, observers are

reminded over and over again just how various the possibilities are for maneuvering when for all the world it looks like confrontation is already at hand. The two sides seem already to have collided; but when you fix your attention on the locus of collision, it turns out an infinitesimal gap still remains, and on either side of this thin sliver of avoidance, the two sides, tensed and flexing, are busy refining and redefining their positions. The moderate leaders on both sides seem to be simultaneously addressing both their opponents and the more hard-line elements among their own constituency. Thus, for example, Prime Minister Jaruzelski calls out the troops, in part, surely, to confront Solidarity with a show of force: but he does it in such a way (small units dispatched to thousands of rural outposts) that you end up thinking it's more a gesture to placate his Soviet overlords and their local clients in the Polish Communist Party. Conversely, Walesa calls an hour-long national strike, in part, surely, to confront the government with the continuing fact of the union's cohesion and determination, but in larger part because he's trying to stem the growing tide of wildcat actions being undertaken by the more radical elements within his own union. Jaruzelski responds by getting Parliament to pass a resolution (one that, admittedly, for the moment lacks any teeth) calling for an end to strikes. Walesa in turn responds by denouncing the resolution and proclaiming that Solidarity will never give up its hard-won right to strike; but within a few sentences, he is pleading with all the wildcat strikers to abandon their actions and return to work. As the month of October comes to an end, Walesa's authority is once again on the line: he is touring the country speaking at one strike-bound plant after another, trying to reassert the union's solidarity and get the workers back to work. It is becoming clear that in the months ahead we will be witnessing a race between the growing frustration of the union's membership and the waning authority of its leadership.

It is raining this evening here in New York. I am remembering the lines in Warsaw, the queues of sad black umbrellas, what rain does when it hits a row of umbrellas, how it drips from one onto the next and then the next, finally streaming into the last person's face and clothes, while his umbrella splatters his neighbor. I am remembering those children in the lines, the water splattering down onto them.

"It's easy for you to come through here with your notepads," my translator scolded me one afternoon after a particularly numbing series of interviews at the Solidarity congress, as we gazed on one such line, "to ask these people your clever questions, to point out their troubling contradictions, to take down your various impressions. In the end you'll pack up and leave, you'll go back to your comfortable office in New York, and type out your report—*but we'll still be here,* trying to see our way through this horrible, horrible winter, and what will your sentences do for us?"

That's fair. That's true.

Another friend told me, the day I was leaving, at the airport: "Oh, Poland, you know, the winter. You American reporters are always coming up with your impossible scenarios. Before it was the Russians, they were going to invade any minute; now it's the winter, no way we'll be able to survive it. You'll see: we'll survive. Winter will come and go, and Poland, miserable Poland, will still be here. Somehow, Poland always persists."

It is raining here in New York, and I am trying to put this manuscript to bed. It does not want to go to bed. Over the radio, I hear reports of a summit meeting between Walesa, General Jaruzelski, and Cardinal Glemp. It occurs to me that not one of these three people—the leaders of the three major institutions in Polish society today—held his position only fourteen months ago. Who knows where they will be four months from now? Who knows where Poland will be?

On my last day in Warsaw, I happened to speak with Neal Ascherson, a fine British reporter who had just been proofing the galleys for his own book, which covers the Polish events up through the Communist Party congress in July. We were talking about how difficult it is to write anything about Poland today that will still be true when it's published a few months from now.

"Yes," he smiled, "but I guess this is what history feels like before it settles, isn't it? It's all wet and squishy and muddy and it gets in your shoes. . . ."

I feel like I've been writing on quicksand.

Epilogue

DECEMBER 1981

"The old is dying, and yet the new cannot be born. In this interregnum, a variety of morbid symptoms appear."

> —Antonio Gramsci
> *The Prison Notebooks*
> (1930)

On the night of December 12, 1981, in a brilliantly executed lightning coup, the Polish military under the command of General Wojciech Jaruzelski imposed martial law on Poland. Within a few days, most of Solidarity's leaders had been herded into detention centers; some placed the total of arrests at over 40,000. Such facts as we have, only two weeks into the new regime, have been collected in the chronology at the end of this book. Precisely because we have so few verifiable facts, this is not the time or place to attempt a history of the recent developments. I want only to provide a few impressions:

There is something profoundly disingenuous in much of the editorializing which has been coming out of the West since the military takeover in Poland on December 13.

Western commentators continually speak as if Jaruzelski's imposition of martial law accomplished some utterly arbitrary emasculation of a healthy, thriving body politic. And yet, I can't imagine a more truthful portrayal of the actual situation in Poland that morning than Jaruzelski's own summation at the outset of his martial law address: "Our country is on the edge of the abyss. Achievements of many generations, raised from the ashes, are collapsing into ruin. State structures are no longer functioning. New blows are struck each day to our flickering economy. Living conditions are burdening people more and more . . ."

The fact is, Poland was probably not going to make it through the winter. Facing imminent famine and a collapse of its health-support systems, the country was lapsing into a state of near anarchy. It's not at all clear that Solidarity had either programmatic solutions or, any longer, the institutional cohesion necessary to develop those solutions.

Where Jaruzelski is being hypocritical, on the other hand, is in his steadfast refusal to accept his own complicity (and that of his moderate colleagues in the Polish Communist Party) in allowing the situation to have deteriorated to this point. There was a time (it was still possible as late as May) when the energies of Solidarity could have been mobilized on behalf of the nation's economic renewal. True, the privileged middle-level bureaucrats, the Red Bourgeoisie, would have had to give up some of their class prerogatives—but given that the alternative was national ruin, perhaps that was not asking so much. Solidarity was willing to negotiate and to compromise—the moderate leaders in Solidarity still commanded enormous prestige and authority, and they would have been able to lead their members along such a path. Instead, they were confronted with endless provocations in the field and boundless bad faith at the negotiating table. The fact that the best Jaruzelski could offer Walesa, as late as this past November, was one seat for Solidarity on an otherwise Communist-controlled seven-member Front of National Accord suggests that the so-called Communist moderates never really had any intention of hazarding a plausible middle solution. Is it any wonder that Solidarity's moderates never had any time to develop programmatic alternatives? In the face of such transparent bad faith on the part of their negotiating partners, they were continually scrambling just to maintain the union's cohesion. By the end, they were even failing at that.

Of course, the question of accountability for the debacle of Poland becomes something like one of those wooden Russian dolls—blame mitigated by still larger blame. Jaruzelski and the other moderates in the Communist party hierarchy most likely could never have negotiated in good faith because of the pressures they were under from their colleagues in the Soviet Politburo. Before we cast the Soviet leaders as the archvillains of the piece, however, it is important to remember that, completely independent of the false issues of Marxist dogma, the hatred between Russians and Poles is centuries old. The Soviet Union lost more than twenty million people fighting the last war on its western frontier. Can any other nation make a comparable claim? Is the Russian reluctance to see a fiercely romantic, potentially violent, and decidedly anti-Russian movement developing at its very border that hard to comprehend? Would the U.S. allow a similar manifestation in Mexico? It doesn't even allow one in El Salvador.

No, in Poland the very land seems cursed. "Geography," my Polish friend told me, "geography dooms us." And it dooms everyone who tries to master its lean imperatives. Jaruzelski's two speeches—December 13 and Christmas Eve—were true masterpieces. From reading them one comes away with the suspicion that this man really felt that he had to act the way he did in order to save the nation. And perhaps he did. "But history," as my friend Daniel Singer commented, paraphrasing Lenin, "doesn't judge by intentions; it judges by results. And it will judge Jaruzelski a butcher." Jaruzelski slaughtered a country's hope and condemned its people to desolation. Many of the country's best citizens were cast to the mercy of brutal prison guards and yet more brutal temperatures. (Jaruzelski may claim that there is still room to negotiate the existence of an independent trade union in Poland, but with whom does he intend to negotiate when the slightest signs of independent thinking have proven grounds for imprisonment?) And he is in the process, apparently, of handing the country back to its worst elements, which is to say the Communist Party or rather that part of the party which has survived the past sixteen months of desertions (there are indications coming out of Poland that Communist Party resignations rose even more dramatically in the wake of the martial law decrees). What remains of the Polish Communist Party as it enters 1982, for the most part, are its least attractive elements: the complacent, the incompetent, the corrupt, and a small but powerful minority of the truly evil—the fascist wing of the party, the perpetrators of the anti-Semitic purges of 1968, Moczar and his crowd. (Recall that as late as March 1981, Stefan Olszowski, one of Jaruzelski's principal heirs apparent in the Communist Party hierarchy and the darling of the Soviet Politburo, was praising the anti-Semitic harangues of the fanatic Grunwald Association.)

So it becomes hard to sustain one's objectivity in considering the deed of Jaruzelski and his colleagues—especially for someone in my position. Many of the people I met in Poland—probably more than half of those I quoted in this book—are today shivering in primitive detention centers. No one knows what will become of them. Granted, I end up feeling, Jaruzelski and his colleagues faced an unenviable set of options; granted, they may have thought they were acting to save the country; granted, if they hadn't acted someone else would have; granted, all of that—still, it is *they* who did act and they who are responsible for the desolation in Poland today.

Retreating from such lofty moral posturings, we should perhaps consider how, in this country with its union of TEN MILLION SOLID, Jaruzelski's lightning coup could have been so remarkably effective at the outset, and then go on to explore the prospects for Poland's new regime in the long run.

As for the first question, three factors stand out. The first involves the nature of the army in Polish society. As late as June 1981, when a poll ranked Solidarity the second most respected institution in Polish society, just after the church, the army came in third, just after Solidarity (the party ranked fourteenth). For Poles, the army is a bastion of nationalist feeling, and a general can legitimately conclude his declaration of martial law by invoking the country's national anthem. And it's even more subtle than that, although it was staring all of us in the face the whole time. "No," my Polish friend had insisted when I asked him whether Polish soldiers would fire on Polish workers. "Look at them, they're just like us. *They are us.*" They are us. And while so many commentators predicted that Polish soldiers would never fight their brothers and fathers and sisters and lovers in the Polish workforce, few acknowledged that by the same reasoning, the Polish workers would never fight them. In any case, as things developed, Jaruzelski was able to keep the issue fairly moot: the army generally was held in abeyance, deployed in noncritical functions—used, for example, to encircle occupied factories but seldom to invade them. That was a task reserved for the highly loyal (and—remarkably—still intact) 56,000-member Internal Security Forces: they did most of the dirty work, one factory at a time.

So, then the question becomes, why didn't the Poles

fight the Security Forces? Presumably there was no love lost between the workers and these minions of the Communist Party. I think the answer is that they would have, back in May. But by December something had happened, something intangible but pervasive. People were so busy speculating on how Poles would behave in the event of an actual civil war that they had failed to notice that one had already started deep within each individual, particular Polish soul. In most Poles, it seems, there is a part which is burningly, heroically, defiantly hopeful and idealistic—but it exists side by side with an aspect which is fathomlessly desolate. Poles *know* that Poland always loses. It is precisely out of the darkness of that knowledge that the flame of their hope still somehow occasionally gleams. Gleams . . . and then gutters out again. By December, the desolation was coming back to the fore, was beginning to drown out the hope. Jaruzelski waited to strike until most Poles already secretly sensed their cause was lost.

Or, phrased another way—and this brings us to our third point—Jaruzelski struck at the very moment when it was most important that individual Poles not be abandoned to their solitary fantasies—and he struck in such a way as to leave them with nothing but those fantasies. Robbed of Solidarity, they were relegated to solitude. "The key to Jaruzelski's strategy," the *London Sunday Times* reported, "was to isolate and thereby neutralize every group, and to deprive them of *any* information, save his own decrees. This was achieved with ruthless ingenuity. Poles could not telephone each other, nor could they write letters, because the post had stopped. They could drive until their fuel ran out—all petrol stations were closed—but not very far, because of the roadblocks. Newspapers, other than government ones, were banned. Sports events were cancelled and small gatherings prohibited. In Gdansk police broke up a queue outside a food shop. In other words, almost every possible forum for ordinary people was banned or obliterated." (Dec. 20, 1981)

Solidarity was a movement which lived by breathing the openness it exhaled. Jaruzelski's brilliant insight was that the way to extinguish the movement was not so much by attacking it directly as by smothering the openness it lived on. For months, everyone had known everything. Now, suddenly, no one seemed to know anything: Were strikes going on? Had there been many deaths? Who and how many had been arrested? Where was Walesa? What was the Pope doing? Nobody knew.

It comes down to something as clichéd as this: Information is light. It was precisely the sudden lack of information that rendered everything so stark. We experienced it here in the West: Without substantive information, the kind we'd become used to, we tended to abandon ourselves to our darkest, most desolate fantasies. *Any information* would have been better than this. Imagine how it must have been for the Poles. No wonder that for the most part, after a few days of resistance, they seemed to crater.

As I write, these last few days in December, two weeks into the new regime, it would seem that Jaruzelski has succeeded in imposing his martial law, for now. The last remaining holdouts, for the time being anyway, are a couple of thousand miners in Silesia. (Think about those miners, by the way, for a moment. Can you imagine what their lot has been for the past two weeks, cooped up like that in those dark, low, primitive shafts, the very walls bleeding a clammy, black, winter dampness—no information, no ventilation, no light, no contact with loved ones, only an abstract terrible sense of the impending future? Poland has an uncanny capacity for secreting such concrete images of its own situation: The country is its own best poet, it is always singing itself.)

But what can Jaruzelski have hoped to accomplish in the long run? Clearly, he hoped that, following the initial shock, he would have been able to get the country back to work, that a touch of military discipline might help pull the country away from the brink of bankruptcy. Indeed, during the first days of the new regime, several Western bankers seemed to share that expectation. "Many U.S. bankers," reported the *Wall Street Journal,* "see Soviet-style authoritarianism as their best hope for recovering the $1.3 billion that Poland owes them." The *Journal* story went on to quote an unnamed bank executive to the effect that "Most bankers think authoritarian governments are good because they impose discipline. Every time there's a coup d'état in Latin America there's much rejoicing and knocking at the door offering credit." (Dec. 21, 1981)

Of course, such expectations quickly proved ludicrously far off the mark. Although Jaruzelski's shock forces were able to break the occupation strike of the mammoth Ursus truck plant just outside Warsaw within its first few days, for example, reports out of Poland this week suggest that during the initial ten days of martial law, the several thousand workers at the plant have produced precisely *one tractor.*

The problem never was getting people to show up for work; it was getting them to work enthusiastically, to boost their productivity. And there doesn't seem to be any way that Jaruzelski's regime will be able to accomplish that. One of Solidarity's first leaflets after the imposition of martial law advised workers in their dealings with authorities to "behave like a halfwit." According to a report out of Gdansk, workers on one side of a ship were busy all right: they were busy unloading all the freight the workers on the other side of the ship were busy loading. Meanwhile, elsewhere, assembly line workers are said to be busily turning out parts that don't match. The entire country is quickly becoming a

Polish joke. The stalemate I saw back in September has merely been carried to a higher level. (I sometimes imagine that if Poland were a chess match, the two masters would have abandoned it a long time ago, declared a draw, shoved the pieces off the board, and started again from scratch. What does one do in a chess match which has achieved stalemate when one's not allowed to quit the game?)

1944, 1956, 1968, 1970, 1976: Poland has been here before. Having soared higher this time, the fall was certainly greater. Solidarity as it existed before December will most likely not return; but neither will Poland roll over and die. Poland keeps coming back. The objective conditions, the internal contradictions which gave birth to Solidarity in the first place still exist in Poland today, and Jaruzelski will not be able to solve them, given the limitations he seems to have accepted for his regime. He and his colleagues may be able to keep the Polish work force down for a few years (at the moment they seem understandably dejected and deflated), but five or ten years from now, the Polish workers will rise again. ("Yes," my friend Anna, a Pole who has just recently emigrated to the United States, agreed when I ventured such speculations to her in a recent conversation, "but it makes me so sad to think it. Imagine: ten years. Young people will become old, old people will die, never seeing victory. It is easy for us here to say, 'Ten years.' They, there, will have to live them.")

At a certain point in a stalemate, the only way out is to change the rules—to add more squares to the board, to allow old pieces new moves—or to suddenly notice that the rules have changed of their own accord. In the long run, Poland may only be sprung from its ongoing stalemate once things begin to move inside the Soviet Union. Perhaps ten years from now, a new generation of Soviet leaders, unformed by memories of Stalin and the war, will be able to allow their satellites a wider orbit. Or else, perhaps they will have become so fixated on their own problems (after all, the kind of class divisions and bureaucratic paralysis which spawned Solidarity are not unique to Poland) that they will not have time to worry about what is going on next door.

We have not heard the last of Poland. And one thing about the Poles—they learn from their mistakes. Right now, in those detention camps, cold men and women are huddling together, whispering, trying to fathom what went wrong, what they did wrong, how to correct for those errors in the future.

For example, they must be thinking, next time we have to attack the security apparatus from the outset. How is it possible that, sixteen months into an extraordinarily widespread political renewal, the party's security apparatus was still intact, virtually untouched, just waiting to be used? "Let him listen," my friend at the Hotel Forum bar had insisted after pointing out a police spy. "Maybe he'll learn something." They did listen, they took their notes. I watched Solidarity members *smile* for their cameras. The police spies bided their time, and now they are having their revenge. Next time . . .

Similarly, next time, the movement's strategists will have to contrive some way of separating the integrity of the national movement from the particulars of each and every local conflict. The entire nation can't be brought to the brink every time some local party bureaucrat provokes a minor disturbance. The local bureaucrats played on that kind of response this time to wear down the union's authority. Next time . . .

And next time, the movement has to be ready to advance concrete economic proposals—specific immediate remedies with short-term possibilities, capable of garnering mass support. This is intellectual work. This time the intellectuals were so intent on letting the working masses take the lead that they tended to shy away from such proposals, preferring to limit themselves to advocating democratic self-governance at the work-place. Next time . . .

For now, the true waiting begins.

For the time being, the Poles have been relegated once again to their longing. It is a longing, centuries old—one which seems to have insinuated itself into the souls of anyone who has tried to live on that low, flat plain. The Chassidic Jews, whose movement was also born there two centuries ago, told wonderful stories about that longing. Elie Wiesel, the survivor of Ausch-witz, recalled one of those stories in his 1970 book, *One Generation After:*

> Having concluded that human suffering was beyond endurance, a certain Rebbe went up to heaven and knocked at the Messiah's gate.
>
> "Why are you taking so long?" he asked him. "Don't you know mankind is expecting you?"
>
> "It's not me they are expecting," answered the Messiah. "Some are waiting for good health and riches. Others for serenity and knowledge. Or peace in the home and happiness. No, it's not me they are awaiting."
>
> At this point, they say, the Rebbe lost pa-tience and cried: "So be it! If you have but one face, may it remain in shadow! If you cannot help men, all men, resolve their problems, all their problems, even the most insignificant, then stay where you are, as you are. If you still have not guessed that you are bread for the hungry, a voice for the old man without heirs, sleep for those who dread night, if you have not under-stood all this and more: that every wait is a wait for you, then you are telling the truth: indeed, it is not you that mankind is waiting for."

The Rebbe came back to earth, gathered his disciples and forbade them to despair:
"And now the true waiting begins."

Or, as Antonio Gramsci, the great Italian communist political theorist, insisted to his followers from the bowels of the prison to which Mussolini had remanded him: This has become a season for "pessimism of the mind, and optimism of the will."

—Dec. 27, 1981

1939–1981
POLAND AND ELSEWHERE
A CHRONOLOGY

A Note on This Chronology

This chronology deals principally with events in Poland since 1939, but I have also included a smattering of references to contemporary events in the United States, Eastern Europe, and the rest of the world. I chose some of the non-Polish dates merely to provide signposts and reference points. Others I chose so as to place Poland's recent history within some kind of context—to avoid the sense, as sometimes prevails when we focus too narrowly on a given subject, that events in Poland were occurring in a vacuum. Thus, for example, the events of 1956 in Poland make a lot more sense when we consider the simultaneous histories of Hungary, the Soviet Union, and the Middle East; similarly, the events at the University of Warsaw in 1968 can be seen as part of the global student movement of the late sixties. I have also provided dates from the recent

American past that help to make Polish history seem both less strange and more remarkable. When we list the various massacres (Poznan, 1956; Gdansk, 1970), it is important to remember that a similar list could be contrived for the United States (Watts, 1965; Kent State, 1970); likewise, the phenomenon of purges, which may seem utterly foreign to us until we recall our own McCarthy era. Some of the American dates (Poletown, PATCO) are therefore provided as an antidote to smugness. Indeed, the history of Poland becomes all the more remarkable when we realize that workers there were for a time able to distill their history of massacres, purges, union busting, and so forth, into precisely the kind of vital, united movement that seems to continue to elude progressives in the United States.*

1939

As the year opens, there are 32,347,000 Poles, of whom 3,351,000 are Jewish. Josef Stalin is sixty years old. Nikita Khrushchev is forty-seven. Leonid Brezhnev is thirty-three. Wladislaw Gomulka is thirty-four. Edvard Gierek is twenty-six and is organizing mineworkers in Belgium. Stefan Wyszynski, who will become Primate of Poland, is thirty-seven. Karol Wojtyla, who will become Pope, is nineteen. Andrzej Wajda is thirteen. Marshal Josef Pilsudski has been dead for four years. It will be four years yet before Lech Walesa is born.

January 30 Hitler requests annexation of free city of Danzig.

---

* In this chronology specific dates (day, month and year) are provided whenever available—in some cases they were not, so the incidents are tagged by month or year alone. Certain types of ongoing movements or cultural events are likewise pegged merely to the year.

1939

August 23 Nazi-Soviet Nonaggression Pact, with secret provisions for the partition of Poland.

August 25 Polish-British alliance.

September 1 Nazis invade Poland, igniting Second World War.

September 3 Britain and France declare war on Germany.

September 17 Nazi Armies reach Brest-Litovsk. Soviets invade from the east, capturing thousands of Polish officers, who will be executed in the Katyn forest (see April 13, 1943).

September 27 Warsaw falls to the Nazis.

September 30 German-Soviet Treaty settles partition of Poland.

October The Germans begin issuing anti-Jewish measures.

1940

The Polish government reconstitutes itself in exile, first in Paris, and then, after the fall of France in June, in London, under the leadership of General Wladislaw Sikorski. Meanwhile, in Poland, various rivalries are sorted out, and the united Home Army (the *Armia Kraieva*), answerable to London, is formed.

April 29 Heinrich Himmler chooses a marshy site for a prison camp in Oswiecim (Auschwitz) in southern Poland. Meanwhile, in Warsaw, the Nazis start supervising the construction of a wall around the Jewish ghetto.

May 20 The Oswiecim town council assigns 200 of the town's Jews to help in building the prison camp. By June, 700 Polish political prisoners arrive.

June 22 The Nazis attack the Soviet Union.

October All Warsaw-area Jews are ordered into the ghetto. Similar measures throughout the country. By

1940

1943, there will be over 500,000 Jews jammed within the walls of the Warsaw ghetto.

December Sikorski flies to Moscow, pleads with Stalin to allow Poles who've fled to the USSR to join the Home Army. Stalin allows formation of a Polish division under General Wladyslaw Anders. Stalin delivers to Anders only 450 of the 9,000 Polish Army officers listed as being held since September in POW camps. He claims the others have escaped to Manchuria. Within a year, Anders's army is transferred to the Middle East; it will fight with the Western Allies there and in Italy (notably at Monte Cassino).

1941

July 30 Stalin reestablishes diplomatic relations with Sikorski's London-based government-in-exile.

September 3 At Auschwitz, first experiments with Zyklon B gas as a mass-extermination agent.

1942

January The Polish Communist Party is revived in Warsaw. Wladyslaw Gomulka is among the early members and takes part in various guerrilla actions.

March 13 First crematorium ready at Auschwitz.

May 12 First trainload of Jews to be funnelled directly into the gas chambers at Auschwitz.

July First major deportations from Warsaw ghetto.

1943

January 18 In Warsaw ghetto, second wave of deportations provokes four days of street fighting. After this, life in the ghetto becomes paralyzed.

February 2 A German army surrenders at Stalingrad.

1943

April 13   The Nazis, in the midst of an eastern-front offensive, uncover the mass graves of thousands of Polish Army officers in the Katyn forest. (Official Soviet and Polish history will subsequently list the corpses as victims of Nazism.) This announcement leads to a rupture in relations between Sikorski's London-based government and Stalin (April 17–25). Stalin starts sponsoring a small alternative People's Army *(Armia Ludewa)*.

April 19   Warsaw Ghetto Uprising begins. Vastly out-numbered Jewish resistance-fighters battle successive waves of Nazi troops.

May 8   The Ghetto Uprising's command headquarters, at 18 Mila Street, falls, although sporadic fighting continues into June. Thereafter, the Warsaw ghetto and most other Polish ghettos are ordered liquidated. Mass deportations begin.

July 4   Returning to London after reviewing the Polish Army stationed in the Middle East, General Sikorski dies in a plane crash. Stanislaw Mikolajczyk becomes head of the London-based regime.

September 29   Lech Walesa is born near Lipno, between Warsaw and Danzig (Gdansk). Within two years his father will be dead from privations suffered in a Nazi prison camp.

November   Wladyslaw Gomulka becomes Secretary of the Polish Communist Party. (Several earlier Party leaders have come to suspicious ends at the hands of both the Nazis and Stalin's agents, but Gomulka will survive the war.)

1944

March   Polish division plays particularly distinguished role in battle for Monte Cassino, Italy.

April   Allied reconnaissance flights over Auschwitz. In

1944

June and July, urgent appeals to bomb the rail lines feeding Auschwitz will go unheeded. The mass extermination of Jews, gypsies, and Poles will continue unabated.

June 25 Admiral Nicholas Horthy, the Hungarian Fascist leader, orders a stop to the deportation of Hungarian Jews, saving thousands.

July 23 The Soviet Army, under Konstantin Rokossovsky, forges across the Curzon Line and into Poland. The Lublin Committee, founded two days earlier and controlled by the Polish Communist Party, declares itself "the sole legal Polish executive power," but the London-based government protests, as do many leaders of the Home Army.

July 24 Polish resistance captures Majdanek concentration camp, near Lublin, and turns it over to the Russians.

August 1 The Home Army launches its own liberation of Warsaw, hoping to secure the capital on behalf of the London-based government. The Soviet Army arrives at the right bank of the Vistula in September and then halts, allowing the Nazis to squash the Warsaw Rebellion, which they do after sixty-three days.

October 2 Warsaw Rebellion collapses. 200,000 Warsovites have died since August 1. Hitler orders the survivors deported and the city razed.

1945

January 17 Soviet Army liberates the ruins of Warsaw.

January 27 Soviet Army liberates Auschwitz. Four million people have been exterminated here, the majority of them Jewish.

February 4–11 Yalta Conference. Roosevelt and Churchill agree to a plan that will subsume the London-based government into a Polish Government of

1945

National Unity, in which the Communists will hold most of the power.

March The Soviet Army has liberated most of Poland. Six million Poles have died during the war. Almost three million Polish Jews have perished (about 350,000 have survived, mostly those in Soviet exile). 38 per cent of Poland's industrial capacity has been destroyed, 35 per cent of its agricultural resources, 30 per cent of its housing stock, and 60 per cent of its schools. Over the next decade, the principal task of the Polish nation will be one of reconstruction.

May 7 V-E Day. The Nazis sign an unconditional surrender.

June 28 The Polish Government of National Unity is transferred from Moscow to Warsaw. Among its twenty-one members, only five are "newcomers," among them Mikolajczyk, who is Vice-Premier. Throughout the summer, however, fighting continues between Polish Communists and the disenfranchised remnants of the Home Army.

August 2 Potsdam Conference. Poland's postwar boundaries are redrawn: in the east, Poland cedes 70,000 square miles to the USSR; in the west, she gains 40,000 square miles from Germany (in effect, the entire country is moved over about 125 miles). Danzig becomes Gdansk and is drained of its German population. Stettin becomes Szczecin. Bromberg becomes Bydgoszcz. These revised boundaries result in one of the largest peacetime migrations in history (eastern Poles to the western part of the country, Germans to Germany). The rootlessness of the citizens of Gdansk and Szczecin (the fact that their residence in these towns is only one generation deep) has been offered by some observers as a factor in their propensity for radical action.

November 11 Marshall Josip Tito's National Front takes power in Yugoslavia.

1946

February 5   Boleslaw Bierut named head of Polish state; Gomulka continues as head of Polish Communist Party.

May 12   Stefan Wyszynski, following a distinguished clerical-academic career and several years of active service in the Underground, is named Bishop of Lublin.

May 26   Communist Party wins parliamentary elections in Czechoslovakia.

July 4   Anti-Jewish pogrom in Kielce, in which Poles kill forty-two unarmed Jews (they had been disarmed the day before by the police). Although this is the most dramatic such instance, hundreds of Jews are being attacked as they attempt to return from concentration camps to their hometowns in Poland, and tens of thousands are fleeing toward Palestine.

November 1   Karol Wojtyla, having spent the war first working in a chemical factory as well as in the Underground, and then in hiding in the home of the Archbishop of Krakow, is ordained as priest and sent to Rome for further studies.

1947

October 5   Warsaw Conference establishes the Cominform (Communist Information Bureau) to coördinate activities of European Communist Parties.

October 12   Mikolajczyk, one of the last holdovers from the London-based regime, is accused of being "an ally of foreign imperialists." He escapes to London on November 3.

October 30   In Washington, D.C., Bertolt Brecht, accused as one of the "Hollywood Eleven" of being a Communist, appears before the House Un-American Activities Committee: he escapes to Europe the next day. He will settle in East Berlin. Committee mem-

1947

ber Richard Nixon will go on to become president of the United States.

1948

February Communist Party seizes complete control in Czechoslovakia; a similar seizure will take place this year in Hungary.

June 24 The Soviets blockade the Allied sectors of Berlin, a blockade circumvented by the Berlin Airlift. Chances for a united postwar Germany quickly fade, and the Soviets begin preparations for a separate East German state.

June 28 Yugoslavia is expelled from the Cominform for hostility to the Soviet Union.

September 3 Gomulka, accused of "nationalist deviations" for opposing collectivization of agriculture, criticizing Soviet domination of the Cominform, and supporting Tito's nationalist line, is replaced as head of the Polish Communist Party by Bierut, on Stalin's orders.

1949

January Following Arab-Jewish war, the state of Israel has consolidated its existence. Many of the Polish Jews who survived the Holocaust have fled to Israel, and the histories of these two nations will continue strangely intertwined for several decades.

January Wyszynski named Archbishop of Warsaw and Primate of Poland (he will be elevated to Cardinal in November, 1952).

January Gomulka relieved of government posts.

March 2 Purge of Czechoslovakian Communist Party.

June 16 Purge of Hungarian Communist Party.

September First Smith Act Trials result in prison terms

1949

for American Communist Party leaders.

October   East German government consolidated under Communist Party control.

October 1   People's Republic of China proclaimed in Peking.

November 11   Gomulka and his allies expelled from Communist Party.

November   Soviet Marshall Rokossovsky changes his name to Rokossowski and, on Stalin's orders, is installed as Polish Minister of Defense.

1950

January 25   Alger Hiss found guilty of perjury for "concealing his membership in the American Communist Party."

February 9   Senator Joseph McCarthy, in the midst of an otherwise routine speech, claims to have the names of 205 card-carrying Communists in the State Department.

April 14   Polish government and the Church sign agreement making provisions for religious toleration and recognizing the Pope as the head of the Church; the Church, in turn, agrees to support the government's foreign policy.

June   Korean War begins.

1951

July   Gomulka arrested as "rightist deviationist" and imprisoned. Countless other arrests and trials.

1952

July 22   Polish parliament approves Soviet-style constitution, institutionalizing "leading role" of the Party.

1953

March 5   Stalin dies of a brain hemorrhage. During the
next several years, there will be a power struggle over
his succession, out of which Nikita Khrushchev will
emerge as leader of the USSR.

June 17   Berlin Workers' Uprising. A protest by 5,000
workers against speed-up provisions leads to a general strike. Two armored Soviet divisions are called
out as the insurgency spreads. The Uprising is finally
put down, with 569 killed and 1,744 wounded.

June 19   In the U.S., Ethel and Julius Rosenberg are
executed for espionage amid a storm of international
protest.

July 23   Armistice at Panmunjom ends Korean War.

September 28   In Poland, Church-State relations take a
dramatic turn for the worse. Cardinal Wyszyinski is
placed under house arrest and will remain so until
1956.

1954

April   Army-McCarthy hearings signal the beginning
of the Senator's fall.

December   McCarthy censured by U.S. Senate.

December   In Poland, Gomulka is released.

1955

May 14   Poland becomes a charter member of the
Warsaw Pact. Polish foreign policy becomes identical with that of Soviet Union. Relations with Vatican severed.

1956

February 14   In Moscow, at the Twentieth Congress of
the Soviet Communist Party, the world Communist
movement is stunned by Nikita Khrushchev's revela-

1956

tion of Stalin's totalitarian excesses. "Rumors" of a vast Gulag turn out to have been true after all. "The cult of personality" is attacked, and the process of de-Stalinization begins.

March 12   No one is more shocked at this turn of events than Stalin's hand-picked Polish leader, Boleslaw Bierut, who dies of heart failure without ever leaving Moscow.

March 20   Bierut is replaced by Edward Ochab at the helm of the Polish Communist Party. Moderates in the Party are busily preparing the way for Gomulka's rehabilitation when they are overtaken by events.

June 28   In Poznan, in west-central Poland, during an internationally attended trade fair, workers at the Zispo engineering factory (formerly known as the Cigielski plant, one of the great proletarian strongholds of the late nineteenth century) go on strike over wage, food, and working-condition demands and march on Stalin Square in the town's center. There, stonewalled by bureaucrats, the demonstrators turn violent, attacking a nearby prison, releasing the prisoners, and commandeering firearms. The authorities respond with tanks, and in the ensuing battle, witnessed by dozens of foreigners, hundreds are injured and as many as seventy are killed. The authorities succeed in suppressing the rebellion, but their own authority has been badly shaken. New leadership is desperately called for.

August 5   Gomulka is restored as a Party member. Moves are under way to return him to the leadership, along with other Communists purged during the early fifties.

October 19   On the Friday morning preceding a weekend Central Committee meeting that will ratify changes in leadership, Khrushchev and other leading Soviet officials arrive in Warsaw, uninvited and unannounced. Soviet armored divisions close in on

1956

the capital. Thirty-six hours of tense negotiations ensue: Khrushchev furiously scolds the Polish leadership, but they do not flinch, and in the end, he does.
On Saturday, the Soviets return to Moscow.

October 21   A Sunday. The Central Committee elects
Gomulka first Secretary of the Polish Communist
Party. "The cult of personality," the new leader tells
the Poles, "was not a matter of just Stalin's personality. This was a system which had been transplanted
from the USSR to nearly all Communist Parties. We
have finished, or rather we are finishing, with that
system once and for all." The situation is still very
tense: no one knows how the Soviets will react. Their
attention, however, is soon distracted by events elsewhere.

October 22   In Budapest, demonstrations that start out
as expressions of support for the Poles take on a life of
their own. Imre Nagy is returned to power and declares Hungary neutral and democratic.

October 24   Soviet troops intervene in Hungary. Following a week of confusion and considerable blood-
shed, the Hungarian Revolution is suppressed. Janos
Kadar is installed as head of the Party.

October 28   In one of his first official acts, Gomulka releases Cardinal Wyszynski.

October 29   While the world's attention is focussed on
Central Europe, Israel (presently joined by Britain
and France) attacks Egypt. The week-long Suez crisis
is resolved on November 5 through a UN Resolution.

November   Poland's "spring in October" continues to
blossom. Soviet Marshall Rokossowski is removed
as Defense Minister. The new leadership sets up a
framework for workers' councils. Meanwhile, there
is a tremendous cultural renaissance: contemporary
art and music festivals, adventuresome novels and
films. Jerzy Andrzejewski publishes *Darkness Hides the
Earth,* a parable about how the Spanish Inquisition

1956

destroyed the people most devoted to Christian ideals. (Arthur Miller's *The Crucible,* a play allegorizing McCarthyism in the form of the Salem witch trials, was staged in the United States in 1953.) Wajda's monumental film *Kanal* chronicles the grim outcome of the Warsaw Rebellion. The dissident journal *Po Prostu (To Put It Plainly)* thrives under such editors as Leszek Kolakowski.

1957

May   Economic Advisory Council urges that individual enterprises be given greater autonomy.

October   As far as Gomulka is concerned, things are getting out of hand. He lashes out at "revisionists" as being worse than "the Stalinist evils they claim to correct." *Po Prostu* is shut down. During the next several months, Gomulka systematically dilutes the authority of workers' councils, subsuming them into the Party-controlled official trade unions.

December 25   The government refuses to broadcast the Primate's traditional Christmas message to the Polish people.

1958

Wojtyla is made Auxiliary Bishop of Krakow.

Wajda's *Ashes and Diamonds* depicts fighting between Communists and remnants of the Home Army, without glorifying the Communists. (The young director is already so internationally esteemed that he is virtually untouchable: he can still risk things that others can not.)

July   Police raid on Jasna Gora monastery at Czestochowa.

1959

Günter Grass, a thirty-two-year-old West German au-
thor who spent the first thirteen years of his life in the
Free City of Danzig (now Gdansk), publishes *The Tin
Drum,* an astonishing first novel which memorializes
Danzig before and during the war. The novel receives worldwide acclaim, and no publication whatsoever in Poland until the late seventies (see May
1977).

1961

January Further deterioration in Church-state relations. Central Committee decides religion can no
longer be taught in the schools. Both sides dig in for a
cold decade.
August 13 East Germans erect Berlin Wall.

1963

June Authorities shut down *Nowa Kultura* and *Przeglad
Kultarlny,* two journals which are among the last ves-
tiges of the spirit of the "Spring in October" of 1956.

1964

April Letter of thirty-four Polish intellectuals calls for
greater freedom of expression; provokes angry official denunciations.
September 29 Free Speech Movement launched at University of California at Berkeley.
November 14 Police search the home of Karol Modzelewski and uncover a 128-page unfinished manuscript; its authors, young intellectuals Modzelewski
and Jacek Kuron, both children of once highly
placed Party officials, are arrested and then released
pending trial.

1964

November 24 Modzelewski and Kuron are expelled from the Polish Communist Party. They subsequently compose and release their "Open Letter to the Communist Party" (based largely on material in the seized manuscript), a detailed critique of Communist practice in Poland that focusses on the tyranny of bureaucratic centralism.

1965

July Trial of Modzelewski and Kuron culminates in three-year sentences for each.

August 11 Watts riots in Los Angeles: 34 dead, over 1,000 injured, nearly 4,000 arrested.

1966

March 31 Pope Paul VI cancels planned visit to Poland (for May 3 ceremony at Czestochowa) as Church-state relations chill further.

June "Cultural Revolution" launched in China: students attack bureaucrats. During the months ahead, Polish police organize demonstrations outside Chinese embassy in Warsaw and ban the import of Mao's "Little Red Book." The Chinese retaliate by showing Nazi newsreels about Katyn inside their Warsaw embassy.

October 21 The Gomulka regime makes no special occasion of the Tenth Anniversary of the launching of Poland's "Spring in October" (ironically, the launching of the Gomulka regime itself), but students at the University of Warsaw do. At a large demonstration, Adam Michnik and other students demand the release of Kuron and Modzelewski. A key speaker at the rally is Lesek Kolakowski, former editor of the journal *Po Prostu* and currently a professor of philosophy at the university.

1966

October 22 Kolakowski is expelled from the Communist Party. Michnik subsequently receives one-year suspension from school.

October 26 Nina Karsov, a twenty-seven-year-old crippled survivor of the Jewish ghetto who has already served fifteen months in prison for political activities, is sentenced to three more years, in a trial that intimates an increasingly virulent anti-Semitism in Poland.

1967

Wojtyla elevated to Cardinal.

June 5–11 The Six-Day War: Israel's stunning victories over Soviet-supported Arab armies lead to an unseemly outbreak of pro-Israeli sentiment on the part of the Polish people. Gomulka's regime, however, like most in Eastern Europe (with the exception of Romania), severs diplomatic ties with Israel. Gomulka warns against Zionist "Fifth Column" within Poland.

July 23 Race riots in Detroit: 40 dead.

September 6–12 French president Charles de Gaulle visits Poland.

October 21–22 End-the-War marches in Washington, D.C. The storming of the Pentagon.

1968

January 5 In Prague, Alexander Dubcek succeeds Novotny as Czech Communist Party First Secretary. By the end of the month, censorship in Prague is suspended, victims of purges are being rehabilitated; a general spirit of liberalization is taking hold, particularly among intelligentsia and *within* the Communist Party.

January 30–31 In Vietnam, the Viet Cong launch

1968

their Tet Offensive and seize American embassy in Saigon.

January 30 In Warsaw, the authorities close down a production of the great nineteenth century Polish Romantic poet Adam Mickiewicz's play "Dziady" ("Forefather's Eve"). The play depicts Poland's suffering at the hands of its czarist Russian overlords, and audiences have been reacting too heartily to certain relevant passages. Students demonstrate at statue of Mickiewicz; one of their leaders, Adam Michnik, is arrested.

March 2 The Polish Writers' Union passes a resolution condemning the state's cultural policy.

March 8 Student demonstrations begin at the University of Warsaw, protesting Michnik's arrest and the closing of "Dziady," along with more general complaints. Among the chants: "All Poland is waiting for its Dubcek!" and "Long live Czechoslovakia!" Demonstrations continue in an orderly manner for the next three days.

March 11 Police and "angry workers" are brought in to quell the disturbances at the University of Warsaw. An eight-hour battle ensues. Among the most violent state forces are the Workers' Militia, organized by Interior Minister Mieczyslaw Moczar, a prominent anti-Semite engaged in a power struggle with Gomulka.

March 12 New Hampshire Primary: Eugene McCarthy 42 per cent, President Johnson 48 per cent.

March 13 An anti-Vietnam march in West Berlin veers in midstream toward the Polish consulate and becomes a solidarity demonstration on behalf of Polish students.

March 14 In Krakow, students launch sympathy strike; such student protests spread throughout Poland.

March 19 Gomulka goes to the airwaves, appeals to

1968

the nation for calm, blames the disturbances on Zionist elements. Moczar launches a series of devastating anti-Semitic purges, of which Gomolka seems to approve (even though his own wife is Jewish). Both the Stalinist fathers and their radical sons come under attack. Of the 30,000 Jews still in Poland, 20,000 will leave within the next few months (many are former Communist Party members and leaders). During this period, a power struggle rages within the Party: Edvard Gierek, the Party chief of the Upper Silesia region, plays a cagey game but generally aligns himself with Moczar and in any case does little to temper Moczar's anti-Semitic activities.

March 25   Kolakowski and five other Jewish professors are dismissed from their jobs at the University of Warsaw.

March 28   A large demonstration at the University of Warsaw demands reinstatement of Kolakowski and an end to the trials of fellow students; the demonstrators give the authorities until April 22 (after Easter recess) to meet these demands. The University responds during the next several days by closing eight departments and announcing that their 1,300 students will have to apply for readmission. All existing student cards are invalidated, and students must apply on a case-by-case basis for new cards.

March 31   Lyndon Baines Johnson announces he will not seek reelection.

April 4   In Memphis, Martin Luther King is assassinated; for the next week, race riots sweep urban America.

April 19   Following Easter vacation in Warsaw, notices are read to all classes that if there are any demonstrations on April 22, the University will be shut down indefinitely.

April 21   Preventive arrests of potential student ringleaders throughout Warsaw.

1968

April 22   There is *no* demonstration at the University of Warsaw. Student troubles subside throughout the country. Kolakowski and many other purged academics leave the country.

April 23–30   In New York City, student dissidents take over administration buildings at Columbia University.

May 2   In Paris, student riots begin outside the Sorbonne.

May 11   In Paris, the Battle of the Latin Quarter reaches its peak.

May 13   Labor unions call for general strike throughout France. Renault headquarters are occupied. Meanwhile, the Vietnam peace talks open in another part of the French capital.

May 19   France is nearly paralyzed by strikes.

May 24   Charles de Gaulle goes to the airwaves to address the nation and turns the tide. He calls for referendum to be held on June 23.

June 5–6   In Los Angeles, Robert Kennedy is assassinated.

June 19–30   Warsaw Pact maneuvers in and around Czechoslovakia.

June 23 and 30   Massive Gaullist victories in French elections. (In the end, as in Poland, the workers do not support the students.)

June 28–30   Violent demonstrations in Berkeley in support of French students.

July   Czech crisis intensifies: the Soviets demand restrictions on press freedom and increased Party discipline.

July 29–August 1   Talks between leaders of Czech and Soviet Politburos.

August 3   Bratislava summit: five Warsaw Pact nations issue statement in which they claim they will respect the sovereignty of the Dubcek regime. Crisis seems to ease.

1968

August 20–21 The Soviet Union and the Warsaw Pact countries (including Poland, excluding Rumania) invade Czechoslovakia. Dubcek and his colleagues are spirited off to Moscow, although they are presently allowed to return to occupied Czechoslovakia.

August 26–29 The Democratic National Convention in Chicago. Police riots ("The Whole World Is Watching"). Hubert Humphrey emerges with the nomination—a Pyrrhic victory.

September 14 Czech government restores censorship.

October 16 Czechs sign treaty agreeing to indefinite placement of Russian troops within Czech borders. Although Hungarian troops participate in the occupation of Czechoslovakia, important reforms are continuing to take place in Hungary itself. Janos Kadar, who was installed by the Soviets in Budapest some twelve years earlier, is proving anything but a tired dogmatist. Taking advantage of Soviet preoccupation with Czechoslovakia during the current year, his regime introduces a series of economic reforms including decentralization of planning, increased trade with the West, and a greater role for the private and semiprivate sector. State-owned enterprises will henceforth be encouraged to make their own decisions on production, and they will be judged on the basis of their profits, which will in turn determine bonuses for workers and managers. As far as the intelligentsia and the cultural community are concerned, Kadar tends to move from a position of "Anyone not with us is against us" to one of "If you're not actively against us, you're with us." Although by no means a paradise of civil rights, Hungary becomes one of the more open countries in Eastern Europe, and the spirit of rebellion evidenced in 1956 begins to fade as the Hungarian economy starts to prosper.

1968

November 5   Richard Nixon defeats Hubert Humphrey in U.S. presidential elections.

1969

Power struggle with Moczar and his allies preoccupies Gomulka; the ongoing purge of liberal elements among the Polish intelligentsia continues; meanwhile, the economic situation of the country worsens.

April 17   In Prague, Dubcek replaced as Party leader by Gustav Husak.

May 15–24   The Battle of People's Park in Berkeley.

July 20   Man on the moon.

August 15   Woodstock Festival draws a quarter million young music fans in upstate New York.

August 19–22   Massive demonstrations in Prague mark first anniversary of Soviet invasion.

September 24   Chicago Conspiracy Trial begins. Eight radicals (of whom one, Bobby Seale, will presently have his case separated from that of the others) are charged with conspiring to incite riots in Chicago in August 1968. The trial, which becomes a media circus, will result in a variety of convictions on February 18, 1970, all of which will subsequently be overturned. Over a decade later, transcripts of White House tapes will reveal a conversation in which Nixon asks H.R. Haldeman, his chief of staff, "Aren't the Chicago Seven all Jews? Davis is a Jew, you know . . . Jerry Rubin . . . Abbie Hoffman. . . . About half of these [radicals] are Jews." Haldeman concurs, "I think more now." Much is made during the trial of the fact that the government is using an arch-reactionary Jewish judge, Julius Hoffman, to preside at this trial of mainly Jewish radicals. (Comparisons are made with the role of Roy Cohn in the McCarthy hearings and Judge Irving Kaufman in

1969

the Rosenberg trial.) A further parallel with contemporary events in Poland can be found in the same May, 1971, presidential conversation. Referring to an upcoming demonstration, Haldeman suggests that they "just ask the Teamsters to dig up eight of their thugs." Nixon concurs, "They've got guys who will go in and knock their heads off." Whether or not an actual order to this effect was ever given, the Nixon Administration does succeed in mobilizing workers, especially the Teamsters and construction workers, against the student antiwar movement.

October 15   Vietnam Moratorium Day.

October 16   The New York Mets win the World Series. Tom Seaver, the winning pitcher, takes out an ad in the *New York Times:* "If the Mets can win the World Series, the United States can get out of Vietnam."

1970

April 30   Nixon announces Cambodian invasion, sparking student strikes throughout the country.

May 4   Four students are killed by National Guard at Kent State; two are killed a few days later at Jackson State in Florida.

June 26   Dubcek expelled from Czech Communist Party.

Fall   Faced with increasing economic difficulties, Gomulka and fellow leaders contrive a new Five-Year Plan that emphasizes an "incentive" system, which in fact will reduce the wages of most workers.

December 13   Growing economic crisis provokes price increases in food (twelve days before Christmas); meanwhile, prices for luxury items are decreased.

December 14   The Lenin Shipyards in Gdansk are bustling. Workers make demands of managers and then, disgusted, march on Party headquarters in the city, where only low Party officials are present. The work-

1970

ers declare a strike. Students at Gdansk Polytechnic, still nursing the wounds of 1968, ignore the workers' pleas that they join them.

December 15   Bloody Tuesday. The workers pour out of the shipyards again, and a free-form battle erupts all over town, culminating in the burning of the city's Party headquarters. The strike spreads along Baltic coast to Gdynia and Szczecin.

December 16   The worst of the tank and helicopter battles in Gdansk takes place on this day.

December 17   The main battle shifts to the Paris Commune Shipyards in Gdynia and the Adolf Warski Shipyards in Szczecin. State of siege throughout the country; Premier Cyrankiewicz addresses the nation.

December 20   Gomulka resigns and is replaced by Edvard Gierek. The battle of the Baltic ebbs; officially, 45 have died, 1,165 have been injured. Unofficial tallies are much higher. Tensions ease during Christmas-New Year holidays.

1971

January 22   New strike in Szczecin over yet another speed-up ploy. Led by ex-sailor Edmund Baluka, the workers demand an audience with Gierek. This leads to an extraordinary nine-hour session in which Gierek insists that "I, like you, am a worker." The strike breaks up with a general sense that the new government ought to be given a chance. Baluka is elected president of the regional branch of the metalworkers' union.

January 25   Gierek meets with representatives of the Gdansk shipyard workers including a twenty-seven-year-old electrician named Lech Walesa.

February 7   Central Committee suspends Gomulka's membership.

February 13   Strikes break out in Lodz (scene of legend-

1971

ary confrontations in 1892 and 1905), led by the women textile workers. They demand—and achieve (on February 15)—a rollback of December food-price increases.

June 24 A revised Five-Year Plan for 1971–75 is announced, marking the beginning of Gierek's economic policy, which emphasizes expansion of the consumer sector based on massive foreign loans.

Summer Crackdown on members of the various December strike committees.

October At a metalworkers' convention, Baluka finds himself the sole delegate among 2,800 who votes against the official resolution. The next day he is sacked from both his union position and Szczecin shipyard job.

December 6–11 Gierek consolidates his position during Sixth Polish Communist Party Congress.

1972

Wajda makes *The Wedding,* a romantic-messianic allegory set in the nineteenth century, in which an intellectual poet marries a peasant and the wedding feast evolves into an armed rebellion against foreign oppressors.

November 5 Richard Nixon handily defeats George McGovern in the American presidential elections. This is perhaps the peak period of Nixon's and Henry Kissinger's foreign policy of détente, which allows simultaneous conduct of war against Communists in Vietnam and vastly increased trade relations with Communists in Eastern Europe (notably Poland, which Nixon visited earlier this year).

1973

The Polish debt to the West is still only $2.5 billion.

1973

Winter   Baluka, the Szczecin activist, is ushered out of the country and settles in Denmark.

October 6–24   The Arab-Israeli ("Yom Kippur") war. In its aftermath, Arab states will embargo petroleum exports to supporters of Israel, resulting in a few weeks of long gas-station lines, spectacular price increases for energy, and the beginning of a long economic slide, which, in turn, will upend Gierek's plans for exporting Polish manufactured goods to prosperous Western markets.

September 11   The government of Salvador Allende in Chile, a democratic-Socialist experiment in the American sphere of influence, is overturned in a violent, CIA-backed military coup.

1974

Dockyard strikes in Gdynia and miners' strikes in Silesia net striking workers various wage increases.

August 9   Richard Nixon resigns from the American presidency in disgrace and is replaced by Gerald Ford, who retains Henry Kissinger as Secretary of State.

1975

August 1   Helsinki Conference on Security and Coöperation in Europe concludes with the signing by thirty-five nations of an Accord that, among other things, recognizes existing boundaries as inviolable and guarantees "fundamental freedoms including freedom of thought, conscience, religion, and belief." Poland is one of the signers.

1976

The Polish debt to the West is now $11 billion.

1976

June 24 Official decree instigates food-price increases of up to 60 per cent. In response, a wave of sit-down strikes sweeps the entire country, notably at the Ursus truck plant outside Warsaw, where workers rip apart a vital train line, and in Radom, site of major armaments plants, where the Party headquarters is torched. Defense Minister Wojcieck Jeruzelski insists that "Polish soldiers will not fire on Polish workers." There are many fewer casualties than in 1970 or 1956, and the Baltic region remains relatively quiet.

June 25 Prices are rolled back, and the strikes sputter out; but beneath the surface, repression is heavy: there are mass arrests of reputed strike ringleaders.

July 23 Peru, on the verge of defaulting on up to $4 billion in debts to private (largely American) banks—thanks in part to economic pressure levied by Western countries against the nascent socialist experiments of its new regime—reaches agreement with a consortium of those banks. The debts are rescheduled on condition that the country adopt a drastic economic stabilization program to be continuously monitored by private bank auditors. In September, still in trouble, Peru receives assistance from the International Monetary Fund, although the IMF exacts even further concessions on Peru's internal economic policies. (See November 10, 1981)

September 23 KOR, the *Komitet Obrony Robotnikow,* the Workers' Defense Committee, is founded by a group of intellectuals, including Kuron, Michnik, and Jan Litynski. According to Kuron, "We were ashamed that the intelligentsia had been silent in 1970 and 1971, and we wanted to restore its good name. After the brutal suppression of workers' strikes and demonstrations, thousands of workers all over Poland found themselves without jobs. Police stations were full. Trials began at Ursus and Radom. KOR set itself the

1976

aim of organizing financial help for people dismissed from work and the families of the imprisoned; of offering legal and—when necessary—medical help; of fighting for freedom for the imprisoned and jobs for the sacked." Founding committee consists of twelve people; at its peak, membership will be limited to just a few more than thirty, so as to avoid police infiltration (although membership lists will be public at all times). Many hundreds of other people will help in unofficial capacities. (Within a year KOR will change its name to KSS, the Committee for Social Self-Defense, although it will continue to be known as "KOR.") The American United Auto Workers extends KOR an initial grant of $10,000.

November 2 Jimmy Carter defeats Gerald Ford in the U.S. presidential race.

1977

January 6 Two hundred and forty Czech intellectuals issue a manifesto calling for greater human rights and form an organization, Charter '77, to monitor the status of those rights in Czechoslovakia. Among the signers are playwrights Vaclav Havel and Pavel Kohut. The Czech regime responds with a wave of severe repression, including several long prison terms in October.

February Wajda's new film, *Man of Marble,* premieres in Warsaw and becomes a huge sensation. The film tells the story of a young contemporary film student's attempt to document the fate of a Worker's Hero of the forties who ran afoul of Stalinist purges during the fifties and then seemed to disappear. A final group of scenes, in which it is implied that the worker died in the 1970 Gdansk massacre, has been cut.

May Several KOR affiliates found NOWA, an underground publishing house—or, not so much a house as

1977

a roving series of basements and attics where activists use primitive equipment and meager supplies to print, collate, and distribute over 200 titles during the next three years. NOWA publications include Orwell's *1984,* Günter Grass's *The Tin Drum,* as well as works by Aleksander Solzhnitseyn and Czeslaw Milosz. The biggest run—over 40,000 copies—will be for a book entitled *What to Do in Contacts with Police.* Even after the events of 1980, NOWA will preserve its underground network of equipment and distribution lest the liberalizing tendencies in Polish society at some point collapse and repression resume.

December Gierek visits Pope Paul VI at the Vatican; this is the culmination of a period of improving Church-state relations, largely engineered by Wyszinski's firm but diplomatic lieutenant, the Bishop of Krakow, Karol Wojtyla. Around this time, following a twenty-year battle, Wojtyla dedicates a church in Nowa Huta, the steel center outside Krakow that the protagonist in Wajda's *Man of Marble* helped to build in the late forties.

December 29–31 Jimmy Carter visits Warsaw and praises the Gierek regime for its relative respect for human rights and religious freedoms. Many commentators feel that the Carter Administration's emphasis on human rights and the Gierek regime's increasing reliance on American goodwill (for debt financing) contribute to a climate in which Polish activists can continue to organize up through 1980. (Harassment is increasingly limited to forty-eight-hour arrests and confiscations of material.) Carter's national security advisor, Zbigniew Brzezinski, and his second Secretary of State, Edmund Muskie, are both of Polish origin.

1978

February "Workers' Committee" (seed of the Free Trade Union of Silesia) formed in Katowice.

May Committee of Free Trade Unions for the Baltic Coast formed, under leadership of Andrzej Gwiazda, including Anna Walentynowicz and Lech Walesa (during this phase, Walesa will later explain, he was "principally a listener").

August 6 Pope Paul VI dies. Wyszinski and Wojtyla travel to Rome to take part in the meeting of the College of Cardinals, which on its first day of balloting selects Albino Luciani, the Cardinal of Venice, as the new Pope. He takes the name John Paul I (Aug. 26).

September 28 His papacy barely one month old, John Paul I dies. Wyszinski and Wojtyla return to Rome for a new meeting of the College of Cardinals.

October 5 Isaac Bashevis Singer wins Nobel Prize for Literature.

October 16 The College of Cardinals, on its second day of balloting, selects Karol Wojtyla, Archbishop of Krakow, as the new Pope. He takes the name John Paul II, as Poles learn in a brief item on the evening news.

December 16 Lech Walesa and Andrzej Gwiazda organize an "impromptu" memorial service at the plaza outside the Lenin Shipyards in Gdansk, site of the 1970 massacre.

1979

June 2–10 Pope John Paul II visits Poland, in his first international foray since becoming Pope, on the occasion of the nine hundredth anniversary of the martyrdom of St. Stanislaw, the country's patron saint. Arriving in Warsaw, he meets with Gierek. Everywhere he goes, hundreds of thousands of Poles rally

1979

to attend his Masses, although media coverage is restrained. On June 4 he visits Czestochowa. On June 7 he visits Auschwitz, where, standing before a Hebrew inscription at a memorial slab, he comments, "The very people who received from God the commandment 'Thou shalt not kill' themselves experienced in a special measure what is meant by killing. It is not permissible to pass by this inscription with indifference." He concludes his pilgrimage in Krakow, where only a year before he was serving as Bishop, and to a crowd of over a million, he says, "Christ will never approve that man be considered, or that man consider himself, merely as a means of production. This must be remembered both by the worker and the employer. . . . Accept the whole of the spiritual legacy which goes with the name 'Poland.' Do not be defeated. Do not be discouraged, and never lose your spiritual freedom."

September *Robotnik,* the underground KOR-affiliated journal, publishes a Charter of Workers' Rights, which will form the basis for many of the Twenty-One Points demanded at Gdansk in August, 1980.

October Founding Committee of the Free Trade Union of Western Pomerania announces itself in Szczecin.

October Over fifty miners killed in three separate explosions in Silesian mines. Workers are angry over working conditions and also over the four-brigade system, in effect since 1978, which mandates six-day shifts at irregular times of day.

October A two-day strike in the Northern Shipyards occurs in Gdansk over an attempt to impose a new wage system.

December 16 Gwiazda and Walesa organize another memorial service for the 1970 martyrs. Many participants arrested. Walesa threatens that if there is no official memorial erected at this site in time for ser-

1979

vices on this date next year, then thirty-five million Poles will bring one brick each and build their own. Officials presumably scoff at the threat.

December 27   Soviet troops invade Afghanistan to shore up friendly regime. One consequence will be an extensive boycott of the upcoming Moscow Olympics. Another will be the fact that as events begin to unfold in Poland, Soviet leaders will find themselves already tied down, to some extent, on this other front.

1980

Spring   In Detroit, General Motors announces the closing of an outmoded Cadillac plant and threatens, in locating its new plant, to abandon the city for a Sunbelt site, unless the city can make a worthwhile counteroffer. Already trying to cope with the high unemployment and huge civic deficits resulting from the ongoing auto industry recession, city officials desperately put together a package including $200 million in enticements and the delivery of a flattened, prepared site. The only trouble is, this plan will require the levelling of the Poletown section of the city, a close-knit community of 3,500 individuals (most of them ethnic Poles, many of them autoworkers), 1,000 homes, and 155 businesses. A Poletown Neighborhood Council forms to fight the rush toward eviction, and the Immaculate Conception Church becomes a center of resistance.

May 3   Small rally in Gdansk celebrates Constitution Day (see May 3, 1981). Two of its organizers are arrested and receive two-month sentences.

June 18   Explosion in the Gdansk shipyards: eight die, sixty are injured. Workers complain of inadequate safety standards.

July 1   It all starts up once again with a government

1980

decree that effectively raises some meat prices by almost 100 per cent. Localized strikes break out almost immediately at factories all over the country. One of the first is at the Ursus plant outside Warsaw, of 1976 fame. Within hours, the strikers are granted pay increases of between 10 and 15 per cent. No sooner do these strikers return to work, mollified, than strikes break out at neighboring plants, with similar pay demands. The pattern continues throughout the month, throughout the country.

July 2 KOR-KSS announces it will henceforth serve as a strike-information clearinghouse.

July 5 With strikes spreading, *Polityka* editor-in-chief Mieczyslaw Rakowski writes, "We must tell the people the truth regarding the disastrous situation of the country. A program of radical reform is urgently needed."

July 10 The notoriously corrupt chief of television and radio, Maciej Szczepanski, of all people, takes to the airwaves to appeal for civic responsibility.

July 11 Managers of important factories confer in Warsaw, are told to buy "social peace" as cheaply as possible but at any price.

The strike spreads to Lublin, near the Soviet border. KOR reports thirty-three factories have been struck thus far, gaining raises averaging 10 per cent.

July 16 Lublin strike by now paralyzes most of city, including, for the next four days, the vital railway link with the Soviet Union. Many Poles feel their meat is being transferred to Moscow for the upcoming Olympics, and such shipments are disrupted. The thirty-five points of the Lublin strike committee anticipate the twenty-one points of the Gdansk strikers, a month hence, without the demand for a free trade union. On July 18, in another anticipation, Deputy Premier Mieczyslaw Jagielski is sent in to negotiate. On July 20, the Lublin strikers accept a

1980

compromise offer—one that the Gdansk strikers will not—and return to work.

July 19 In Moscow, the Summer Olympics begin, badly truncated by the boycott of many Western nations protesting the Soviet incursion into Afghanistan. The Olympics will continue through August 3.

July 21 Workers in Radom (another site of 1976 trouble) are given unsolicited pay raises to prevent strikes.

July 26 Strikes have now affected one hundred enterprises.

July 27 Gierek leaves for a three-week working vacation, by Leonid Brezhnev's side, in the Crimea.

July 29 The first small strikes break out on the Baltic coast.

July 31 Lech Walesa placed under the last of a ten-year series of forty-eight-hour arrests.

August 1 On the thirty-sixth anniversary of the outbreak of the Warsaw Rebellion, 4,000 Warsovites gather in the Powazki Cemetery to pay homage to the victims of Katyn.

August 2 At 3 A.M., the youngest of Lech and Danuta Walesa's six children is born; her father is released from jail at 10 A.M.

August 3 The Moscow Olympics conclude.

August 4 Warsaw garbage collectors go out on strike.

August 5 Three dissident activists, including Jan Litynski, editor of *Robotnik,* are arrested and then released shortly thereafter.

August 6 Anna Walentynowicz, a dissident activist and crane operator at the Lenin Shipyards, whom the authorities have been trying to sack for years (she and KOR have been fighting the attempt in court), goes home ill. The next day she is dismissed for "deserting her work post."

August 8 KOR expresses its willingness to serve not only as an information agency but also as a contact center

1980

for various strike committees. Since July 1, 150 factories have been struck.

August 9 In Gdansk, a small party celebrating the release of the two activists jailed May 3 is attended by most of the local Free Trade Unionists: they discuss the possibility of launching a strike on behalf of Anna Walentynowicz. The next day, a delegation drives to Warsaw to discuss possibilities with Kuron and other KOR leaders.

August 11–14 In the United States, this is the week of the Democratic National Convention. Carter defeats Kennedy, provoking a walkout by some union leaders, including the Machinists' William Winpisinger. At this point, hostages have been held in the American Embassy in Teheran for over nine months, a fact with which the American media and people are obsessed.

August 11 First known arrest of a strike leader (a Warsaw garbage collector) during this round of troubles. In Gdansk, 6,000 leaflets setting out the initial strike demands are printed during the night.

August 12 In Warsaw, the Politburo propaganda chief tells Western reporters that the labor unrest has passed its peak, though isolated strikes are still occuring.

A new 1.2 billion *deutsche mark* loan is announced by twenty-four banks. An American-led consortium moves ahead with an additional $300 million loan agreement. (The Polish debt to the West now exceeds $20 billion.)

August 14 5,000 Warsovites gather at the Tomb of the Unknown Soldier on the eve of the sixtieth anniversary of his death, which occurred during the heroic defense of Warsaw by a nationalist army, under Marshal Jozef Pilsudski, against an invading Soviet force (1920).

Meanwhile, in Gdansk, the pace abruptly quick-

1980

ens: the 16,000 workers at the Lenin Shipyards stage an all-out strike beginning with the morning shift. Initial demands include the erection of a memorial to the 1970 martyrs; reinstatement of three recently fired fellow workers, including Walentynowicz; a wage increase of 2,000 zlotys (the average salary is 5,500 zlotys per month); and the right to form an independent union.

Tadeusz Fiszbach, the local Party Secretary, arrives. Negotiations are being broadcast live over the P.A. system, as they will be for the duration of the strike. Walentynowicz is brought to the shipyard and permitted to address the workers. Lech Walesa secretly scales the shipyard walls. The workers close off the plant and refuse to leave.

August 15   Communications blackout: all phone lines to Gdansk are cut. In the town, transport is suspended. Over 50,000 workers are on strike.

Gierek returns from the Crimea, a week early.

Prime Minister Edward Babiuch addresses the nation on television, cites "our allies' concern."

Cardinal Wyszynski, delivering an Assumption Day address at Czestochowa, makes an oblique reference to the situation: "Bread is the property of the whole nation," and Poles are asking for it "in a tactful way, in a way full of dignity."

Soviet TASS news agency announces routine maneuvers of Warsaw Pact armies in East Germany and Baltic areas.

August 16   False reports of the strike's resolution almost sabotage the workers' united resolve: Walesa himself wavers, initially accepting concessions on the monument, reinstatement of fired workers, and a big pay increase. Within moments, realizing that many workers are willing to stay out for more, he changes his mind. But the strike leaders no longer have access

1980

to the loudspeakers. In the nick of time, Alina Pien-
kowska, a shy, soft-spoken nurse from the shipyard
infirmary, reaches the gates, shouts out to the departing workers to stay, and the strike is saved. Fourteen
days later, the workers will accept smaller pay raises
in exchange for other, more substantial concessions.

Meanwhile, an Interfactory Strike Committee
(MKS) is established in Gdansk to coördinate and represent the rapidly spreading strike actions.

August 17   An open-air Mass at the shipyard gates.
Gdansk Bishop Kaczmarek sends medals of Pope
John Paul II to members of strike committee.

Deputy Prime Minister Tadeusz Pyka is named
head of a government delegation and sent to Gdansk.

Litynski is placed under house arrest again; Kuron
is cautioned.

August 18   Gierek cancels trip to West Germany.

August 19   Strike spreads all along Baltic coast, notably to Szczecin, where parallel but separate negotiations are launched. Walesa emerges as leader of the
Gdansk MKS. Students at Gdansk Polytechnic contribute 10,000 zlotys to shipyard strike fund.

August 20   Fourteen KOR activists arrested, including
Kuron and Michnik.

August 21   Jagielski (see July 16) replaces Pyka as head
of government delegation. MKS now consists of 500
delegates from 261 striking factories with a fifteen-
member presidium. Twenty-four activists have been
arrested.

August 22   Pope offers Mass for Poland.

MKS, which now represents 400 factories, publishes
the first issue of its mimeographed daily bulletin in
the shipyard printing plant: It is titled *Solidarnosc.*

August 23   Jagielski arrives at Lenin Shipyards, is
presented with Twenty-One Demands. Talks end in-
conclusively. MKS demands restoration of communi-

1980

cations links to rest of country as prerequisite for further talks.

August 24 In Warsaw, Central Committee meeting results in firing of Prime Minister Babiuch (he is replaced by Jozef Pinkowski). Stefan Olszowski and Tadeusz Grabski—who, during the year ahead, will become leading hard-liners—move up in the Politburo. Maciej Szczepanski is relieved of his duties at Polish TV. Gierek, for the moment, survives.

August 25 MKS will not resume talks: communication links have not been restored.

Seven experts, including lawyers and economists, arrive from Warsaw to assist MKS negotiating team. Fiszbach expresses confidence in strikers' good intentions.

Late this night, communications are restored.

August 26 Second round of talks with Jagielski. MKS delegates now number almost 1,000.

Portions of a sermon given by Cardinal Wyszynski at Czestochowa are broadcast over Polish TV. It appears the Cardinal is urging the workers to respond to the government's appeal that they return to work, although the Church subsequently expresses outrage at the selective editing of the sermon by the broadcasters.

August 27 Third round of talks with Jagielski.

August 28 Walesa appeals for temporary halt ("three or four days") to spreading strikes, to allow negotiators time to achieve agreement.

August 30 The negotiations reach their climax. Breakthrough reported in Szczecin in the late morning, in Gdansk a few hours later. Jagielski returns to Warsaw to report to the Central Committee, which presently ratifies the agreements. Andrzej Wajda, on a visit to the shipyards, is told, "Now you must tell our story, Man of Iron!" He will accept the challenge.

1980

Meanwhile, some additional arrests are reported.

August 31   Jagielski returns to Gdansk. Some confusion remains as to the applicability of these accords for the rest of the country and the fate of the arrested dissident activists. As for the latter, strikers demand their release and Jagielski promises to do what he can. Walesa promises that workers will go back on strike if release does not come quickly.

Government and strikers sign final agreement in large conference hall at the shipyard. A crucifix hangs on the wall, and Walesa uses a giant souvenir pen with an image of the Pope. Essential points include sanctioning of a free, independent union with the right to strike; improved health and working-condition standards; Saturdays off; allowing Masses to be broadcast over the radio; loosened censorship and political repression.

Walesa: "We have shown that Poles can come to an agreement if they want to." Jagielski: "We have spoken as Poles to Poles."

First group of detained activists released.

September 1   Strikers in Gdansk and Szczecin return to work. Strikes continue elsewhere in the country, as workers are unsure if the Gdansk provisions apply to them.

Remaining dissidents released.

Lech Walesa takes possession of the new union's Gdansk office.

September 2   5,000,000 zlotys have already been received in donations to the new free trade union. National press publishes full text of the accord, placing words like "censorship," "political prisoners," and "privileges of Party members" in quotes.

September 3   Agreement with 350,000 strikers in Upper Silesia, Gierek's home district.

In Rome, Pope John Paul II speaks of Poland's moral right to independence.

1980

USSR grants Poland further loans and food supplies.

September 4 Exposé released on financial misconduct of media-czar Szczepanski.

Pope's speech reported in Polish media.

September 5 Parliament meets: very open and critical debate. First secretary Gierek is absent: it is reported he has been hospitalized due to heart trouble. Late-night meeting of Central Committee: Gierek is ousted as Party Secretary and replaced by Stanislaw Kania (previously in charge of, variously, the Army, the Secret Police, and relations with the Church).

September 7 Walesa attends private Mass in Warsaw at home of Cardinal Wyszynski.

September 8 As strikes sputter on, the new Party leaders tour the country.

September 8–15 The Seventh Annual Festival of Polish Feature Films in Gdansk includes screenings of several previously suppressed documentaries (films that will be transferred, in repertory, for extended runs at Warsaw's Non-Stop Kino) and a special midnight showing of rushes for *Robotnicy '80 (Workers '80)*, Andrzej Chodakowski's and Andrzej Zajackowski's documentary of the August strike. Walesa attends the screening, flanked by the Vice Minister of Culture and the Archbishop of Gdansk.

September 11 Jagielski briefs Brezhnev in Moscow.

September 15 The authorities declare the Gdansk accords applicable to the entire country, pending official registration of the union by the courts.

September 21 For the first time since the Second World War, Sunday Mass is transmitted throughout the country by radio.

September 22 For the first time since July 1, there are no strikes in Poland. The delegates of thirty-six regional independent unions meeting in Gdansk unite under the name "Solidarity."

1980

During this period, Karol Modzelewski emerges from academic seclusion (he has been a professor of medieval studies at Wroclaw University) to become official national press spokesperson for the union.

September 24 Solidarity attempts to register with Warsaw court, as required by law. Court takes the registration under advisement; during the coming weeks, the court's delay in formalizing the union's existence will lead to increasing tension.

October 3 Solidarity stages a nationwide one-hour warning strike to protest the government's failure to honor many of the wage settlements achieved in August and to demonstrate the union's strength. The demonstration is tremendously effective, and the strike receives extensive coverage on the TV evening news.

October 9 Czeslaw Milosz, Polish poet and essayist living in exile in the United States, is awarded the Nobel Prize for Literature. His works, largely unavailable in Poland, will begin to appear by way of the various "underground" presses, and he will quickly become a national hero.

Meanwhile, in Warsaw, a substantial cabinet shake-up.

October 24 The crisis escalates sharply when the Warsaw court makes registration of Solidarity's charter contingent upon the union's inclusion of language in the charter recognizing "the leading role" of the Communist Party. Solidarity, which has done all the recognizing it cares to do in this regard in its August 31 agreement, refuses to include such language in its charter and sets a November 12 deadline for resolution of the problem—or the union will call a general strike. Walesa sets union membership at eight million.

October 29 East Germany announces severe travel restrictions on travel between the two countries.

1980

Throughout the coming months, the East German leadership will take an even dimmer view of Polish developments than do the leaders in the Kremlin: the East Germans sense themselves caught between capitalist and revisionist states.

October 30 Kania and Pinkowski are in Moscow consulting with Brezhnev. Wyszynski is in Rome (as he will be for a total of seventeen days), consulting with Pope John Paul II.

October 31 In Detroit, the city council, by a vote of 8-to-1, decides to level Poletown.

November 4 Ronald Reagan defeats Jimmy Carter in the American presidential elections.

November 8 Romania's Nicolae Ceausescu warns against foreign interference in Poland.

Wyszinski returns from Vatican.

Growing sense of impending crisis as Solidarity's November 12 general strike deadline approaches.

November 10 Polish Supreme Court rules that the charter legalizing Solidarity can stand without reference to the leading role of the Communist Party. Solidarity withdraws strike threat.

November 12 Senate of the University of Warsaw apologizes to the victims of the 1968 anti-Semitic purges.

November 14–18 Crisis in Czestochowa is averted when a hard-line provincial governor, objectionable to Solidarity elements, resigns.

November 21–24 Crisis in Warsaw. Two Solidarity printers are arrested, and workers at their factory, the Huta Warsawa steelworks, threaten to strike. Walesa and Kuron rush over to mediate, and the crisis subsides when the printers are released. Walesa appeals for an end to the wave of wildcat strikes. Hard-line bureaucrats, however, keep concocting provocations that lead to local flare-ups.

November 22 Communist Party shakeup at local level

1980

> sees ouster of at least eighteen of forty-nine first secretaries.

November 29 Students at the University of Warsaw end a sit-in after the authorities agree to the registration of an independent student organization.

December 1 Soviet Union declares the area between East Germany and Poland a "restricted military zone" for the next ten days and forbids visits by foreign tourists. During the first half of December, tensions increase steadily and Western governments make their most worried pronouncements yet as to the dangers of an imminent Soviet invasion.

December 3 Nine European-community nations issue warnings; Carter speaks of increasing concern.

December 5 Surprise meeting of Warsaw Pact leaders in Moscow: Kania is accompanied by hard-liner Stefan Olszowski.

December 7 Carter Administration warns that the Soviets have completed military preparations for invasion.

December 10 Italian Communist Party warns Soviets against invasion.

December 12 Polish Catholic Church condemns acts by political dissidents and extremists (implying KOR) "that could raise the danger of a threat to the freedom and statehood of the fatherland."

> Secretary of State Muskie is in Brussels where NATO officially warns USSR of the consequences of an invasion.

December 13 Kania says Poland must be left alone to resolve its own problems.

> For no reason in particular, tensions begin to ebb. By December 15, Soviets are suggesting that they are content for the moment to let the Polish Communist Party handle things; they complain that U.S. is "fanning war psychosis."

1980

December 14   In Warsaw, 1,000 farmers from through-out the country gather to press their demand for regi-stration of their own union, Rural Solidarity.

December 16   In Gdansk, the dedication of the memo-rial to the 1970 martyrs (a towering monument con-sisting of three crosses with anchors crucified atop each, which has been designed and built by the work-ers inside the shipyard), on the occasion of the tenth anniversary of their deaths, provides an opportunity for an unusual show of unity; representatives of Soli-darity, government, and Church attend.

mid-December   Mieczyslaw Moczar has been making a steady comeback in the Polish Politburo since the fall of his rival, Gierek. A group of intellectuals call for the government to examine the question of anti-Semitism and, specifically, the 1968 purges in which Moczar had such a notorious role.

December 20   Kuron criticizes Church for its implicit attacks on KOR back on December 12th.

December 31   At year's end, Poland's debt to the West has increased to $23 billion, and the government is emphasizing the scarcity of food and other supplies in urging an end to labor unrest.

1981

January   Throughout the month, the authorities and Solidarity are engaged in a confrontation over the question of the five-day, forty-hour work week: the government wants to grant two Saturdays a month off, Solidarity insists on all Saturdays off. A second major issue concerns the registration of a parallel farmer's organization, Rural Solidarity, which is staging a sit-in in Rzeszow that lasts most of January and continues into February.

January 12   *Robotnicy '80,* the documentary film detail-ing the Gdansk strike of August (see September 8,

1981

1980), premieres in Warsaw, moving on to a tremendously successful semi-underground run throughout the country.

January 14–20   Walesa leads a Solidarity delegation to the Vatican for various audiences with the Pope. In addition, the delegation visits Monte Cassino (see March, 1944) for a ceremonial wreath-laying, and Walesa visits with his stepfather, who makes the trip from the United States.

January 20   Ronald Reagan inaugurated President of the United States; Alexander Haig becomes Secretary of State. Iran hostages released.

January 24   As part of ongoing conflict over the five-day work week, Solidarity simply has its membership take this Saturday off.

January 25   Gierek accepts a modicum of responsibility for his ten-year rule, although he transfers most of the blame onto associates; he asks to be relieved of his seat on the Central Committee, and is obliged.

Increasing number of wildcat strikes during this week, notably a ten-day general strike in Bielsko-Biala over the question of an objectionable provincial governor.

January 30   Agreement on the issue of the work week, which is to become five-day in 1982, although in 1981 workers will still work a few occasional Saturdays.

February 3   Solidarity plans a one-hour strike to demand that the government negotiate with the farmers in Rzeszow; the strike is called off when the government sends in a negotiating team. Throughout the month, Walesa lends his prestige to these ongoing negotiations at various moments. The talks are being documented by filmmakers in what will eventually become *Chlopi '81 (Farmers '81)*.

February 7   Wyszynski receives a delegation from Rural Solidarity.

1981

February 8 Government announces inquiry into KOR.

February 9 Prime Minister Pinkowski is dismissed and replaced by Defense Minister General Wojciech Jaruzelski (see June 24, 1976).

February 10 Polish Supreme Court ruling seems to preclude registration of Rural Solidarity but leaves some room to maneuver.

February 15–17 Kania meets with his counterparts Gustav Husak in Czechoslovakia and Erich Honecker in East Germany (the two leaders most critical of Poland's course).

February 17 Rural Solidarity suspends Rzeszow sit-in as talks continue.

February 23 The Soviet Communist Party Congress in Moscow. Kania and Jaruzelski attend; Brezhnev is relatively reticent on the subject of Poland.

March 8 At the University of Warsaw, 3,000 faculty members and students commemorate the anniversary of the 1968 demonstrations and protest anti-Semitism.

Meanwhile, in front of a nearby building that used to house the Ministry of Public Security, an association known as Grunwald stages a rally of 500 people, with speeches attacking Stalinist Jews of the forties and fifties for torturing Polish patriots, and condemning dissident Jews affiliated with KOR today for once again leading the nation astray. The rally is favorably reported in the official media and is praised by hard-liner Olszowski. Solidarity vehemently condemns the development.

March 9 In Poznan, Rural Solidarity, still officially unrecognized, holds its first congress.

March 11 Large-scale Warsaw Pact maneuvers, *Soyuz '81,* announced for late March.

March 13 Polish Catholic bishops' congress again warns Poles not to be exploited by extremists (implying KOR).

1981

March 17 Strike averted in Radom when two objectionable officials resign.

Moczar, pandering to Polish nationalism once again with a different strategy, says he will seek to return the ashes of General Sikorski (see 1940–43) from London to Polish soil. Some see this as a government ploy to try to divert the growing popular cult of Pilsudski.

March 19 A sit-in in Bydgoszcz by Rural Solidarity is broken up in a violent display of police force: dozens are hurt, and three are hospitalized, including Rural Solidarity leaders Mariusz Labentowicz and Jan Rulewski. Posters featuring photographs of the two injured activists go up all over Poland. Solidarity declares a nationwide strike alert and demands that those responsible for the attack be disciplined.

March 20–30 A period of ever-increasing tension. As the Warsaw Pact begins its *Soyuz '81* maneuvers, Walesa and Deputy Prime Minister Rakowski (see July 5, 1980) hold vital negotiations on Bydgoszcz situation.

March 27 Solidarity holds four-hour warning strike as it continues to mobilize toward a threatened general strike on March 31. During this period, there is perhaps the greatest sense of an impending Soviet invasion since the beginning of the crisis.

March 30 At the last moment, Walesa reaches a compromise with Rakowski and railroads a cancellation of the strike through his national commission.

Meanwhile, at a stormy meeting of the Communist Party's Central Committee, hard-liners Grabski and Olszowski are on the verge of being voted off the Politburo when a strongly-worded letter from the Kremlin stays the purge. The Politburo remains unchanged.

March 31 In Washington, D.C., Ronald Reagan is shot but survives the assassination attempt.

1981

April 1 Furious outcry within Solidarity at the lack of democratic process in the climactic Bydgoszcz negotiations which culminated in the suspension of the strike; also criticism of the compromise itself, in which no one was even reprimanded for his role in the police violence (a study committee was established). Karol Modzelewski resigns as press spokesperson and returns to Wroclaw. The beginnings of serious rifts within Solidarity. Meanwhile, national meat rationing begins.

April Edmund Baluka, the Szczecin activist from the early seventies, returns to Poland.

April 2 Jagielski is in Washington, D.C., negotiating emergency aid with Vice President Bush.

April 4 During the early part of the month, Secretary of State Haig and Secretary of Defense Caspar Weinberger continue to warn of the extreme danger of Soviet intervention in Poland. Haig at the same time is busy intervening in the internal affairs of El Sálvador, a country within the American sphere of influence.

April 6 In Prague, at the Czechoslovakian Communist Party Congress, as Brezhnev listens, Husak warns that the Warsaw Pact will not watch passively as the Communist system in Poland is undermined. Poland is represented at the conclave by Olszowski, not Kania. On April 7, Brezhnev says he still believes Poland's leaders will be able to solve their own problems. Later in the day, completion of the *Soyuz '81* maneuvers is announced.

April 10 Polish parliament approves a resolution calling for two-month suspension of strikes and citing extreme economic constraints.

April 15 Meeting of local Communist Party delegates in Torun calls for democratic changes within the Party.

April 17 Government accedes to demands of Polish

1981

farmers for creation of Rural Solidarity, pending court registration in May.

April 26 Western governments agree to rescheduling of Polish debt payments; Western banks continue to negotiate. Total debt now exceeds $25 billion. Polish passport regulations liberalized.

April 30 The Central Committee of the Communist Party, in its seventh meeting since August, calls for a July 14 emergency full Party Congress to be preceded by an open delegate-selection process (using secret ballots).

April 30 In Poletown, Detroit, the Immaculate Conception Church is deconsecrated. Much of the neighborhood has already been razed, although activists continue to use the church basement as their headquarters. Water, gas, and electricity for the church are shut off, but the activists remain.

May 1 In Warsaw, an unusually scraggly and small demonstration marks the official celebration of May Day. Rationing, meanwhile, is extended to a wide variety of products besides meat.

May 3 Massive celebrations throughout the country mark the one hundred ninetieth anniversary of Poland's constitution. In 1791, during the period of the French Revolution, the Poles temporarily held off the process of their successive partitioning by rallying under this document (a remarkably liberal charter that freed the serfs, widened the voting franchise, and extended civil rights to Jews). After 1919, with the establishment of an independent Polish state, May 3 became the national holiday, although its observance was suspended after 1947.

May 9 Crowd in the Warsaw suburb of Otwock, furious over police treatment of two drunk youngsters, torches the police station. Solidarity and KOR leaders rush over to calm the crowd. Lech Walesa leaves for week in Japan as guest of Japanese trade unions,

1981

whose worker-participation systems he has praised.

May 10   Francois Mitterand wins French presidential election. Within a month, his Socialist party will sweep the assembly elections.

May 12   Warsaw court registers Rural Solidarity.

May 13   At the Vatican, Pope John Paul II is shot and seriously wounded. Stunned Poles watch extensive coverage on their televisions. The situation is particularly tense because, at the same time, Cardinal Wyszynski has fallen seriously ill.

May 26   Two former Gierek ministers commit suicide as corruption investigations broaden.

May 27   Wajda's film *Man of Iron,* completed only a few weeks earlier, and approved by the Culture Ministry—without cuts—only a few days earlier, wins the Golden Palm at the Cannes Film Festival.

May 28   Cardinal Stefan Wyszynski dies at age seventy-nine. His funeral procession three days later draws hundreds of thousands, including Communist Party and Solidarity leaders.

June 3   Soviet TASS news agency begins favorably quoting the statements of a mysterious hard-line Polish Communist group that calls itself the Katowice Forum.

June 5   Walesa addresses International Labor Organization in Geneva.

June 6   Tadeusz Fiszbach, the Gdansk Communist Party leader, attacks Party hard-liners, such as those in the Katowice Forum, for their recalcitrance. Some consider him a possible candidate for Party First Secretary at upcoming Party congress.

June 7   Czeslaw Milosz, Nobel laureate, returns to a hero's welcome in Poland: he receives honorary doctorate at University of Lublin and later in the week visits the 1970 Memorial outside the Gdansk shipyards, where a verse from one of his translations of the Psalms has been engraved on a facing wall.

1981

June 10 Central Committee meeting, and yet another Soviet-sponsored attempt to remove Kania is yet again repelled (this time Kania suggests separate votes on each Politburo member, and the hard-liners quickly retreat).

June 13 Walesa denounces the defacing of a Soviet war memorial in Lublin and orders Solidarity workers to clean the monument. The defacement is one of the first overtly anti-Soviet gestures in what up till now has been an extremely self-disciplined movement.

June 21 In a poll released in *Kultura* magazine, Solidarity ranks as the second most respected institution in Polish society, immediately behind the Catholic Church. The Communist Party ranks fourteenth. The Army is third.

June 28 In Poznan, 150,000 attend memorial service for 1956 martyrs, including dedication of a monument consisting of two crosses.

July Roman Polanski makes a triumphant return to Warsaw, starring in the title role of his own stage production of Peter Schaefer's *Amadeus.*

July 7 Bishop Jozef Glemp of Warmia is named by Pope John Paul II, who is still recuperating from his gunshot wounds, to succeed Cardinal Wyszynski as Primate of the Polish Church.

July 9 Labor trouble shifts to LOT, the state airline, where workers strike for four hours; their choice for manager has been passed over by the government, which considers the position of national security importance. Troubles persist through much of the month.

July 14 In Warsaw, an extraordinary congress of the Polish Communist Party takes place, in which 2,000 delegates, elected through a free and secret balloting process, themselves vote to use secret balloting in elections for Party leadership—a first in the history of

1981

the Soviet bloc. As the congress proceeds, however, the two extremes (represented by Fiszbach and Rakowski on the one side and Grabski and Olszowski on the other) tend to cancel each other out, and the leadership that emerges, with Kania still at its head, is moderate and, if anything, nondescript.

Meanwhile, in Poletown, Detroit, the basement of the Immaculate Conception Church is emptied of its last remaining defenders, and the church is razed to the ground, symbolizing the end of the Battle of Poletown. Within a few months, most of this once-thriving community will be paved over as a parking lot for the new General Motors Cadillac plant.

July 27   In Warsaw, Wajda's *Man of Iron* is released, uncensored.

July 25–August 10   With food lines lengthening and supplies dwindling precipitously, food protests erupt throughout Poland. Solidarity tries to stem the growing anarchy as it prepares, through a nationwide delegate-selection process, to convene its own first annual congress in September. The authorities, meanwhile, in the wake of the Communist Party congress, launch a withering media attack on the anti-Socialist elements within and aspirations of the Solidarity leadership.

August 3   In the United States, 12,000 air-traffic controllers strike over wage issues and working conditions. President Reagan, who has had nothing but praise for striking workers in Poland, summarily fires all 12,000 (August 5) and moves to decertify their union (PATCO). The American labor movement pays lip service to the need for solidarity but fails to take substantive united action. The only real support the air-traffic controllers do receive comes from foreign (Canadian, French, Portuguese) controllers.

August 19   In Poland, wildcat strikes by printers start up in protest to the government's anti-Solidarity me-

1981

dia offensive. Solidarity-government negotiations focus on the question of access to media.

mid-August Kania goes on *his* Crimean vacation at Brezhnev's side.

August 26 In the wake of the government's media campaign and in light of anxieties about the coming winter, some polls show a drop in Solidarity's popularity.

August 27 A strike in Radom Province is averted when authorities agree to compensate workers injured in the 1976 disruptions.

August 29 Solidarity wins limited media access: a panel of four Solidarity speakers, including Walesa, is granted twenty minutes on TV on the evening of September 1, as the union's national congress nears; but subsequent negotiations will fall through.

August 31 Poles observe the first anniversary of the accords that ended the Gdansk strike. Solidarity now claims almost ten million members, all of whom have been canvassed in the delegate-selection process leading up to the congress, in itself an incredible achievement for a year-old organization.

September Eighth Annual Gdansk Film Festival surveys the year's production of Polish films (along with some older films that have only recently been permitted public release). Highlights include Bohdan Poreba's *Polonia Restituta,* a long historical drama on the fate of Poland during and immediately following World War I; Janusz Kijowski's *Index* and Janusz Zaorski's *Dziecinne Pytania (Childish Questions),* two films dealing with the disillusionment of the student generation following the repression of 1968; and Piotr Szulkin's *Wojna Swiato (The War of the Worlds: Next Century),* with the Russians, more or less, in the role of Martians. Andrzej Petrokowski's documentary of the negotiations that culminated in the recent registration of Rural Solidarity, *Chlopi '81 (Farmers '81),* re-

1981

ceives a last-minute, midnight public screening, although judging from the angry reactions of Culture Ministry officials, it is still an open question if the film will ever be granted a general release. Agnieszka Holland's *Goraczka (Fever),* a tale of Polish terrorists and their attempt to bomb czarist Russian representatives during a stillborn 1905 nationalist insurrection, receives the Festival's Grand Prize.

September 4 Soviet Navy launches war games off Poland's Baltic coast.

September 5 850 representatives from throughout the country convene in Gdansk for the first session of Solidarity's First National Congress of Delegates. Archbishop Jozef Glemp, the new Primate of Poland, opens the congress by celebrating Mass at a nearby cathedral. Lech Walesa, in his opening remarks, wonders whether Solidarity and the authorities will continue to talk "like a Pole to a Pole" (see August 31, 1980). Polish television, which has refused to grant Solidarity its own slots in covering the convention, is banned from the hall.

September 5–7 A prison break and takeover in Bydgoszcz result in a tense standoff, which Solidarity's intermediaries rush to defuse.

September 5–10 The first session of the Solidarity congress proceeds in Gdansk. Walesa beats back an attempt to undermine the authority of the union's central leadership bodies. The union attacks the "worker self-management" bill currently before the Polish parliament as a charade and demands a national referendum to decide between that bill and Solidarity's version; should the government fail to hold such a referendum, Solidarity will hold its own. The congress also calls for more open and authentic voting procedures in next year's parliamentary elections. Finally, on September 8, the congress votes to send a letter of greeting and support to workers and

1981

free trade unionists throughout the Soviet Union and Eastern Europe. The delegates subsequently adjourn the first session for two weeks of consultations in their home districts.

September 11 Moscow describes the first session of the Solidarity congress as "an anti-Socialist and anti-Soviet orgy." Workers at the huge Zil truck plant outside Moscow are shown on Polish and Soviet television approving an angry counterletter denouncing Solidarity.

September 12–22 Although the Soviets end their Baltic naval maneuvers, tensions in Poland mount dramatically. The Communist Party unleashes its fiercest attacks yet on the union. Soviet leaders send their Polish counterparts an extremely tough letter, portions of which are released on September 18. Rumors suggest that the unreleased portions include threats of drastic cutbacks in delivery of such raw materials as petroleum. A poll taken during this period and released at the end of the month suggests that 40 per cent of Poles expect a violent resolution to the crisis in the near future. Many fear that the government will attempt to cancel the second session of Solidarity's congress. Against this background, Solidarity and government officials continue to negotiate the "worker self-management" issue.

September 15 The Vatican releases a papal encyclical entitled *Laborem Exercens (On Human Work)* in which John Paul II echoes many of Solidarity's positions. (All property "is acquired first of all through work in order that it may serve work." For that reason, the means of production "cannot be possessed against labor ... because the only legitimate title to their possession—whether in the form of private ownership or the form of public or collective ownership—is *that they should serve labor.*" [Pope's italics])

September 19 In Washington, D.C., approximately

1981

250,000 march in an AFL-CIO-sponsored "Solidarity Day" protest against Reagan's economic policy. A substantially larger throng gathers in New York City's Central Park for a Simon and Garfunkel reunion concert. In the United States, as opposed to Poland, labor and the sixties generation have not yet found each other.

September 22 A poorly attended meeting of Solidarity's presidium votes three-to-one (Rulewski is the only dissenting vote) to accept a "worker self-management" compromise and cancel the call for a referendum. Three days later, the parliament approves the compromise, which allows some worker input in the selection of managers but reserves exclusive Party control at key security enterprises. Tensions ease somewhat.

September 26 The second phase of Solidarity's congress opens with angry attacks on the leadership for its failure to observe democratic process in the recent "self-management" negotiations. The discussions are reminiscent of the controversy of late March and early April. Finally, its energy spent, the congress votes a mild reprimand of the leadership and then fêtes Walesa on the occasion of his thirty-eighth birthday. Presently, the congress will agree, with certain reservations, to honor the compromise.

September 28 At the Solidarity congress, Edward Lipinski, the ninety-three-year-old economist who is KOR's spiritual leader, announces the committee's disbanding. Henceforth, KOR activists will simply serve as members of the union. To tumultuous applause he claims that it is the government, not KOR or Solidarity, that is anti socialist.

October 2 Walesa defeats more radical opponents (Andrzej Gwiazda, Jan Rulewski, and Marian Jurczyk of Szczecin) for the chairmanship of the union, although he garners only 55 per cent of the vote. The

1981

congress goes on to elect a national commission considerably more radical than its chairman.

October 3 During the congress's last days, Solidarity offers a two-year economic program of its own and suggests it may convene a "people's tribunal" to try cases of corruption that the government seems unwilling to confront. Bogdan Lis, the union's number-three leader, suggests that Poland limit military spending as part of its economic recovery plan.

October 4 The government announces steep price increases on food and tobacco; Solidarity reacts with outrage. Tense negotiations ensue.

Mid-October Wildcat strikes over the food-price increases and supply shortages erupt once again all over the country; women textile workers outside Warsaw are especially militant.

October 15 Solidarity wins a temporary price rollback and freeze as negotiations continue.

October 18 Under increasing pressure, Stanislaw Kania resigns as Communist Party First Secretary. In an apparent rebuff to hard-liners, however, the Central Committee selects Kania's moderate associate, Prime Minister (and Defense Minister) General Jaruzelski to succeed him. Jaruzelski, who now holds all three positions, joins the Central Committee in proposing a ban on strikes.

October 19 Walesa finds himself opposing both a strike ban and the strikes the ban would ban.

October 20 Police in Katowice provoke violent street demonstrations by arresting, at the busiest time of day and in the middle of the city's busiest square, three Solidarity activists distributing literature exactly as they have been doing for months.

October 23 Jaruzelski sends Army troops out into the countryside; but the initial panic that his announcement engenders subsides as it becomes clear that the units are being deployed in groups of three and four,

1981

principally to help local rural administrators with food collection and distribution.

October 24   Twenty-fifth anniversary of Soviet invasion of Hungary. The Hungarian economy is currently the most prosperous and stable in Eastern Europe, thanks to the program of reforms launched in 1968.

October 28   Solidarity stages a one-hour nationwide strike. Both Jaruzelski and Walesa indicate that they hope it will be the last, but it isn't.

early November   Workers at the Sosnowiec coal mines in Lower Silesia, having found traditional work stoppages counterproductive in solving the political impasse, contrive a decisive innovation: "the active strike." They continue working, but they set their own hours, manage the mine themselves, and supervise distribution of their product—in this case coal, which they send to small farmers and day nurseries.

November 1   Thousands gather in Powazki Cemetery in Warsaw on All Saint's Day to commemorate the martyrs of Katyn.

November 4   An unprecedented summit meeting brings together the leaders of the three most powerful institutions in Polish society—Solidarity's Walesa, the Party's Jaruzelski, and the Church's Glemp.

Not one has been in office longer than eighteen months, and all three together may no longer have enough authority to see Poland through its current crises (Walesa's own national commission takes advantage of his absense to censure his autocratic style), but they agree to continue talks.

November 7   Most extensive ongoing strikes since Solidarity's inception continue in Zielona Gora province in dispute over fired activist. 160,000 are off the job and 200,000 more threaten despite national Solidarity leadership's urgings to contrary.

November 8   In Moscow, sixty-fourth–anniversary celebration of Bolshevik Revolution.

1981

In Prague, Czech Prime Minister Strougal announces balance-of-trade difficulties with both Western and Communist-bloc trading partners.

November 9 Solidarity, insisting on its willingness to meet the government halfway, releases a six-point agenda for future talks: (1) social control of economic decision-making, (2) access to mass media, (3) economic reform, (4) democratization of local government at district and province level, (5) reform of legal system, and (6) price reforms.

The government, for its part, proposes seven-member "front of national accord," with Solidarity to have one seat, the party to have another, and five of the party's alter-egos to have the other five.

November 10 Student strikes spread throughout country in support of students at Radom Engineering College who oppose the selection of the newly appointed rector.

Poland formally applies for membership in the International Monetary Fund in hopes of gaining access to fresh lines of credit to help in meeting debts to Western banks. U.S. and West Germany approve and the Soviet Union suspends its earlier veto. IMF negotiation will require several months and will involve a virtually complete audit of the national economy.

November 11 For the first time since 1939, Poles mark anniversary of their country's rebirth as an independent nation at the end of World War I in ceremonies which commemorate the memory of Marshal Josef Pilsudski.

November 12 Although the twenty-two–day wildcat strike in Zielona Gora ends, over 250,000 Poles are now on strike elsewhere.

November 13 New economic figures released by the government show Polish industrial production in October 1981 down yet another 15 percent from the

1981

year before, and exports to the West down 25 percent.

November 15   Solidarity's Silesia branch calls upon its members to begin selecting candidates for local government councils.

November 17   In the first substantive talks in over three months, Communist Party and Solidarity officials meet in Warsaw to consider the possible formation of a "Front of National Accord." During the next few days, the parties agree on an agenda for the talks but little else.

The most prolonged and unusual protest in the nation, a "sit-in" by eleven escaped convicts on top of the 140-foot smokestack of a power station at the Zaleze prison in southern Poland, enters its sixteenth month.

Soviet officials acknowledge a labor dispute at the Togliatti Lada plant 600 miles south of Moscow in 1980.

November 18   President Reagan attempts to derail the growing West European nuclear disarmament movement by offering a proposal—the so-called "zero-option"—which at first glance seems bold but at second seems less so.

November 19   Polish army announces surprise withdrawal of the hundreds of small military units which were surprisingly sent into the countryside on October 23.

November 21   In Amsterdam, 350,000 demonstrate against the nuclear arms race; 200,000 also do so in Romania.

November 22   Leonid Brezhnev travels to Bonn for consultation with Chancellor Helmut Schmidt.

Polish police raid home of Jacek Kuron, break up a meeting, but make no arrests.

November 23   Fifteen prominent Solidarity members, including Andrzej Gwiazda (although no one from

1981

the union's ruling presidium), resign from their positions to protest Walesa's "too conciliatory stand"; similar resignations in Rural Solidarity.

November 24 Marshal Viktor Kulikow of the Soviet Union, commander of the Warsaw Pact forces, in Warsaw for consultations with Jaruzelski.

November 25 Three hundred firefighter cadets occupy training school in Warsaw, striking for academic rights and exemption from police activities. The government, which considers firefighters a component of the military establishment, is extremely disturbed and stations police around the building.

November 26 The government and Solidarity have become stalemated in their talks, which have failed to move beyond the agenda item on economic cooperation. Politburo hard-liner Stefan Olszowski rejects Walesa's proposals that Solidarity be given veto power on the decisions of any cooperative council.

November 27 Politburo instructs government to seek emergency legislation, among other things banning strikes, and notes that in twenty-one of the forty-nine provinces attempts have been made to eliminate Communist Party organizations at factories.

November 29 Jaruzelski tells the Communist Party Central Committee that "a state of war" is imminent if there is no quick end to strikes.

November 30 US-USSR arms-reduction talks open in Geneva.

December 2 Helicopter-borne Warsaw police raid the firefighters' academy and forcibly remove the 300 cadets, provoking angry denunciations by Solidarity. During this operation, Solidarity's telex and telephone communications in the Warsaw area are temporarily disrupted.

During this period Poland is represented at a meeting of Warsaw Pact defense ministers by General Florian Siwicki, who will become an important

1981

member of Jaruzelski's military government in less than two weeks. (Siwicki led Polish forces in Czechoslovakia in 1968.) Soviet General Kulikow pays several visits to Warsaw during the days ahead.

December 4 Two hundred-and-eight-billion–dollar military spending bill passes U.S. Congress—largest in history.

December 5 Walesa and Archbishop Glemp meet to discuss deteriorating political situation in wake of December 2 police action.

Rural Solidarity proposes merger of its union, Solidarity, and the student union into one great movement.

Support strikes on behalf of students at Radom Engineering School now idle 70 of Poland's 104 institutions of higher learning.

December 6 Warsaw regional Solidarity sets December 17 as day of protest against the December 2 police action which ejected firefighter cadets and urges entire national union to go along. In addition, Warsaw Solidarity calls on national leadership to establish a force of "permanent worker guards to ensure that we are adequately protected in the future."

December 7 Warsaw radio asserts that tape recordings of closed Solidarity leadership meeting in Radom include passages where Walesa and others predict imminent confrontations and advocate overthrow of the government. Walesa confirms he made such remarks but says they have been taken out of context. Meanwhile, the talks leading to a national unity coalition remain stalled.

December 8 Archbishop Glemp appeals to Walesa and Jaruzelski to resume their dialogue.

December 10 Soviet leadership fires off yet another anxious and anxiety-provoking note to the Polish Central Committee.

Walesa, under heavy pressure from his national

1981

commission, comments, "We do not want confrontation but we cannot retreat anymore. We cannot be passive any longer as this would be detrimental to the union."

In Chile, on Human Rights Day, seven prominent dissidents, including three members of the Chilean Human Rights Commission, are arrested and turned over to military courts—the latest such detentions in eight years of unrelenting repression.

December 11 At its national commission meeting in Gdansk, Solidarity serves notice that it will stage a twenty-four–hour nationwide strike if the government passes laws giving itself extraordinary emergency powers (such as that of banning strikes). Rulewski of Bydgoszcz calls for speedy elections to all representative institutions, and Jurczyk of Szczecin calls for free elections to parliament no later than March 31, 1982. A Solidarity leader from Legnica raises objections to the presence of Soviet troops and their huge base in his home district.

Meanwhile, the Polish government asks French Prime Minister Maurois to postpone his three-day visit scheduled to begin December 16.

Elsewhere, Helmut Schmidt of West Germany opens three days of talks in East Germany with his counterpart, Erich Honecker, the first such high-level talks between the two Germanies since the end of World War II.

And in Detroit, the United Auto Workers executive board, under heavy industry pressure, votes to allow revising (and downsizing) of previously negotiated contracts.

December 12 Film Polski, at the last minute, submits *Man of Iron* as its nominee for the American Academy Award. Ironically, the film's director, Andrzej Wajda, is on this very day apparently being detained. Once considered untouchable, he will be

1981

unable to protect the dozens of people under his patronage during the week ahead. They, too, are thus suddenly exposed and subject to arrest.

Meanwhile, in Gdansk, Solidarity's national leadership votes to endorse its Warsaw chapter's December 6th call for a nation-wide day of protest on December 17th. In addition, as Walesa looks on in frustrated silence, the commission takes its most radical—and some feel most provocative—action yet. They vote to hold a February referendum in which the entire country will be canvassed for its opinion on four questions:

(1) Are you in favor of a vote of confidence in General Jaruzelski?

(2) Are you for establishing a temporary government and free elections?

(3) Are you for providing military guarantees to the Soviet Union in Poland?

(4) Can the Polish Communist Party be the instrument of such guarantees in the name of the whole society?

When, a few hours later, the assembled delegates receive word that communications are being cut, Walesa angrily rebukes his fellow leaders: "Now you've got the confrontation you've been looking for."

December 13 The eleventh anniversary of the beginning of the bloody week of martyrs in Gdansk and the other Baltic coast towns (1970).

During the night between Saturday, December 12, and this Sunday morning, troops take up positions all over Poland, sealing off city after city. All internal telephone and telegraph lines are cut. In Gdansk, police round up the Solidarity leaders gathered in town for their national commission meeting. Lech Walesa refuses to leave his house until Tadeusz Fiszbach, the Gdansk party first secretary, whom he trusts, is present. Fiszbach arrives, Walesa leaves,

1981

and is spirited off to Warsaw. He will not be heard from in person for some time. Throughout the country, in lightning raids, Solidarity's regional leadership is being arrested—as are intellectuals, cultural figures, journalists, even some priests.

Poles awakening to a dazzlingly clear morning, the first after two weeks of cold, gray skies, learn of the imposition of martial law as they turn on their radios, which are endlessly replaying General Jaruzelski's 6 A.M. address to the nation. Invoking emergency constitutional powers, Jaruzelski declares a "state of war" and places the government under the direction of a twenty-one–man Army Council of National Salvation. Army generals and commissars will take over all government ministries, although Jaruzelski insists these emergency measures will only be temporary. He concludes by quoting the national anthem, "Poland is not yet lost as long as we yet live."

In an attempt to soften the blow, the government announces the arrest of four former Communist Party leaders, including Gierek, who are held responsible for the current economic debacle. These will be joined by twenty-three others on December 15. But many of those supposedly detained will apparently surface in Moscow within the week.

The military regime, insisting that there will be "no turning back from socialism," issues a series of twenty separate martial law decrees, including: 1) temporary suspension of basic civil rights such as freedom of press, speech, assembly, access to communication; 2) banning of all public gatherings, including demonstrations, strikes, sports and artistic events (all theatres, movie houses, and dance halls are closed), with the sole exception of religious gatherings; 3) institution of a curfew from 10 P.M. to 6 A.M.; 4) banning of distribution of any publications or use

1981

of any printing equipment, including office copying machines, without prior government approval; 5) sanctioning of mail and telephone censorship and eavesdropping; 6) requirement that all Polish citizens carry ID cards at all times and not leave the place of their official residence for more than forty-eight hours without permission; 7) sealing of all Polish frontiers and closing of Polish airspace to all commercial flights; 8) restriction of all TV and radio broadcasts to one Warsaw-based channel; 9) closing of all educational institutions, with the exception of nursery schools, for an indefinite period; 10) "militarization" of police, fire, civil defense and thousands of national-security–related industries so that workers become subject to military discipline; 11) authorization of armed forces to use "coercion to restore calm, law and order"; and 12) authorization of summary proceedings in the case of any violators of martial law (with penalties ranging as high as death).

The 56,000-member Internal Security Forces (ZOMO), paramilitary security forces particularly loyal to the party, are placed on alert and deployed in three regions—Warsaw, Northern Poland, and Southern Poland. It is they who will undertake the brute work of strikebreaking and coercion; the army will be called on principally to encircle trouble spots into which ZOMO troops will then be injected.

Solidarity, as much of it as survives the blitz, calls for a general strike.

John Paul II is the first Westerner to learn of the takeover. In a 1 A.M. phone call, he is told by Polish diplomatic representatives in Rome of Jaruzelski's impending move and he is given various assurances which turn out in the next few days to be false. They serve their immediate function, however, by helping to assuage the Catholic hierarchy inside Poland.

1981

Archbishop Glemp in his morning sermon appeals to Poles not to resort to violence: "Do not start fighting Poles against Poles."

West Germany's Schmidt, still in East Germany, avoids comment on the Polish situation and declines to cut short his trip.

December 14 Telex lines of four Western news agencies are cut; a complete and astonishingly effective news blackout ensues.

[*NOTE: Owing to this news blackout, the remainder of this chronology, which was being prepared during the last week in December, can only be described as tentatively accurate in its account of events from this day forward.*]

Defiant workers stage strikes in major industrial centers throughout the nation as work is supposed to begin on this Monday morning. Mines in Silesia, the Ursus and Huta Warsawa steel mills outside Warsaw, the shipyards in Gdansk and Szczecin, and countless other factories are occupied by their workers and then encircled by government troops. Further arrests are proceeding. The government will eventually claim a total of 4,000 detentions, with Solidarity sources quoting ten times that figure.

Western bankers meeting in Paris to decide on future rescheduling of Poland's debt (the meeting had been called before the current crisis) initially express hope that the military takeover in Poland will lead to a quick resumption of normal working conditions which will enable the government to acquire the hard currency necessary for meeting its debts.

The U.S. suspends $100 million in economic assistance.

Meanwhile, in Israel, Prime Minister Menachem Begin, a Polish Jew, takes advantage of the world's

1981

distraction with events in Poland to annex the Golan Heights, reminding some observers of Israel's behavior back in October 1956.

December 15   One by one, the government is crushing individual strikes—by which is meant, the ZOMO forces are evicting the occupying workers *and not letting them back in.* When workers are eventually allowed to return, they engage in slowdown tactics and passive resistance. Thus, although the mammoth Ursus plant outside Warsaw is once again operating by mid-week, it produces only one tractor during the first ten days of martial law. With phone lines between cities cut, any pretensions toward industrial efficiency vanish.

A police raid on the National Academy of Sciences in Warsaw leads to arrests of hundreds of intellectuals.

Tremendous quantities of food start appearing at Polish markets as the military regime tries to convince Poles that things are getting better and only succeeds in convincing them that the government was hoarding food all along, thereby helping to induce the crisis.

The black market rate for dollars shoots from 400 to 700 zlotys in a single day.

December 16   The eleventh anniversary of the worst violence in Gdansk 1970, a day upon which commemorative services have been planned for some time.

During the predawn hours, ZOMO forces attempt to break the shipworkers' occupation at the Gdansk yard and are to some extent successful; but during the day, thousands of Gdansk citizens converge on the memorial plaza just outside the shipyard gates, where widespread fighting ensues, resulting in hundreds of injuries, although the government insists no deaths.

1981

Seven deaths do occur, however, as the government itself admits, during violence that day at the Wujek mine in Silesia.

Warsaw radio broadcasts a list of fifty-seven interned dissidents including Edmund Baluka, Andrzej Gwiazda, Marian Jurczyk, Jacek Kuron, Jan Litynski, Tadeusz Mazowiecki, Adam Michnik, Karol Modzelewski and Jan Rulewski. Also on the list are three Solidarity leaders who turn out to be in Europe and America, thereby suggesting that the list was made long before the actual crackdown.

Archbishop Glemp begins to take a harder line, calling for an end to martial law, freeing of prisoners, revival of labor unions—and national prayer.

In a move of dubious efficacy, the U.S. State Department retaliates against the grounding of American diplomats in Poland by restricting movement by Polish diplomats inside the United States to within twenty-five miles of their consular offices.

December 17   Further violence in Gdansk; and in Warsaw, a tear-gas attack on demonstrators seeking sanctuary in the Church of the Holy Cross.

December 18   As the situation is beginning to "normalize," Solidarity strongholds have been reduced, according to government accounts, to a section of the Gdansk shipyard (which the workers have wired with explosives), a steel mill and a few mines in Silesia. Glemp smuggles out a letter to Paris in which he says Poles are living through a reign of terror.

December 19   Jaruzelski, the only Soviet bloc leader not personally in attendance, cables Leonid Brezhnev thanks for his help and understanding during the current crisis, on the occasion of the Soviet leader's seventy-fifth birthday celebration in Moscow.

December 20   Romuald Spasowski, Polish ambassador to the United States, complaining that "a cruel night

1981

has spread over my country," defects to the United States in his "expression of Solidarity with Lech Walesa."

December 21   At least 2,800 miners are still barricaded deep inside two Silesian mines in what is becoming a harrowing vigil.

December 22   Western banks in Paris categorically reject Poland's request for $350 million to be applied toward interest due them by December 31.

The government announces a lifting of the curfew for Midnight Mass on Christmas Eve. The Polish Communist Party Politburo meets for the first time since the proclamation of martial law.

December 23   With the miners' strikes continuing, negotiations between Church and Communist Party officials are said to commence.

President Reagan, on national television, insists that, "The Soviet Union through its threats and pressures deserves a major share of the blame for the developments in Poland," and then aims the bulk of a package of fairly ineffectual sanctions against Poland. (Poland couldn't afford to buy any of the embargoed products anyway.)

December 24   General Jaruzelski addresses the Polish nation stating that there remains a place for independent trade unions in Poland (despite the fact that virtually all the leaders of the only one that currently exists are being held in detention centers under reportedly frightful conditions). "The transitional burdens, rigors, and restrictions" of martial law are "decisively a lesser evil than the fratricidal conflict which not long ago stood on our threshold."

The Polish ambassador to Japan defects to the United States.

A Vatican envoy arrives in Warsaw from Rome to meet with Jaruzelski.

1981

   The striking miners ignore government pleas that they join their families for Christmas. Poles throng to Midnight Masses throughout the country.

December 25   Christmas comes to this overwhelmingly Catholic country, like a cruel joke.

The 21 Demands

These are the 21 Demands which the Interfactory Strike Committee (the MKS) presented to government representatives on August 23, 1980, in Gdansk, and which formed the basis for the negotiations that culminated in the agreements of August 31, 1980.

1. Acceptance of Free Trade Unions independent of both the Party and employers, in accordance with the International Labor Organization's Convention number 87 on the freedom to form unions, which was ratified by the Polish government.
2. A guarantee of the right to strike and guarantees of security for strikers and their supporters.
3. Compliance with the freedoms of press and publishing guaranteed in the Polish constitution. A halt to repression of independent publications and

access to the mass media for representatives of all faiths.

4. (*a*)   Reinstatement to their former positions for: —people fired for defending workers' rights, in particular those participating in the strikes of 1970 and 1976; —students dismissed from school for their convictions.

   (*b*)   The release of all political prisoners (including: Edmund Zadrozynski, Jan Kozlowski, and Mark Kozlowski).

   (*c*)   A halt to repression for one's convictions.

5. The broadcasting on the mass media of information about the establishment of the Interfactory Strike Committee (MKS) and publication of the list of demands.

6. The undertaking of real measures to get the country out of its present crisis by:

   (*a*)   providing comprehensive, public information about the socio-economic situation;

   (*b*)   making it possible for people from every social class and stratum of society to participate in open discussions concerning the reform program.

7. Compensation of all workers taking part in the strike for its duration with holiday pay from the Central Council of Trade Unions.

8. Raise the base pay of every worker 2,000 zl/per month to compensate for price rises to date.

9. Guaranteed automatic pay raises indexed to price inflation and to decline in real income.

10. Meeting the requirements of the domestic market for food products: only surplus goods to be exported.

11. The rationing of meat and meat products through food coupons (until the market is stabilized).

12. Abolition of "commercial prices" and hard currency sales in so-called "internal export" shops.

13. A system of merit selection for management posi-

tions on the basis of qualifications rather than Party membership. Abolition of the privileged status of MO, SB [Internal Security Police], and the party apparatus through: equalizing all family subsidies; eliminating special stores, etc.

14. Reduction of retirement age for women to 50 and for men to 55. Anyone who has worked in the PRL for 30 years, for women, or 35 years for men, without regard to age, should be entitled to retirement benefits.

15. Bringing pensions and retirement benefits of the "old portfolio" to the level of those paid currently.

16. Improvement in the working conditions of the Health Service, which would assure full medical care to working people.

17. Provision for sufficient openings in daycare nurseries and preschools for the children of working people.

18. Establishment of three-year paid maternity leaves for the raising of children.

19. Reduce the waiting time for apartments.

20. Raise per diem from 40 zl to 100 zl and provide cost-of-living increases.

21. Saturdays to be days off from work. Those who work on round-the-clock jobs or three-shift systems should have the lack of free Saturdays compensated by increased holiday leaves or through other paid holidays off from work.

NOTES

1. As for the situation of Western banks vis-à-vis Poland, there's an old Eastern European Jewish story that applies. Schlomo can't sleep one night; he's tossing and turning and itching and squirming, and finally his wife says, "Schlomo, what's wrong? You're driving me crazy with all this tossing." And Schlomo says, "Tomorrow's Friday." "So? So tomorrow's Friday. So what?" asks his wife. "Well, I owe Moishe ten rubles on Friday, and I don't have the money." "Ah, Schlomo," sighs the wife, climbing out of bed and heading toward the window. "Here, I'll take care of that." She opens the window, leans out into the still night air, and yells, "Hey, Moishe!" Across the way, a few moments later, Moishe's window creaks open. "Yeah," the old man grumbles, "what do you want at this crazy hour?" "Moishe," says the woman, "tomorrow's Friday." "Yeah, I know. So what?" "Well, Schlomo owes you ten rubles tomorrow." "Yeah, I know, so what?" "Listen," says the woman. "He doesn't have the money. He's not going to pay you." Whereupon she closes the window and returns to bed. "There," she says to her husband. "Now, *you* sleep and let *him* stay up all night worrying."

Or as one economist explained the situation for me: "When you owe the bank one hundred dollars and you can't pay them back, you're in big trouble. When you owe them a hundred million dollars and you can't pay them back, *they're* in big trouble."

In this case, as we have seen, the money owed is over twenty-five billion dollars, and it's owed to a consortium of over one thousand Western banks (principally American and West German). As of May, though, these banks were not exactly suffering. Poland has been rescheduling its debt, but none of the debt has been cancelled, and rescheduling merely means that Poland pays money now for the privilege of being able to forestall its payments on the principal until later. In other words, Poland will end up paying the banks substantially more in total than it would have had it been able to meet the initial schedule. The banks will do fine, so long as Poland doesn't default completely.

Some people wonder why Poland doesn't just default and refuse to honor its debts. "I suppose they could do so," one Western economist told me, "but then the country would be reduced to the status of a leper, a pariah among nations. No one would ever extend Poland credit again—it would be virtually impossible for an industrialized nation to proceed in an environment of such isolation. No, for all their exposure, the banks have Poland nailed."

2. When portions of these essays first appeared this past November in *The New Yorker,* this section on Jewishness and anti-Semitism in contemporary Poland evoked the strongest response among the readership—at least as far as I can gauge from the ensuing correspondence.

One man from New Jersey wrote: "Worse than an anti-Semite is an anti-Semitism apologist. Only a Jew could find a historical rationale for his own persecution. To claim that anti-Semitism is not deeply rooted in the Poles since they recognized the lie in Russian propaganda about Solidarity being a Zionist plot insults Polish intelligence. Until the Poles admit their cruelty to others and accept differences within their nation, they will never treat each other fairly. The Germans have at least expressed regrets for their treatment of the Jews. As far as I have seen, there is nothing of the kind coming from the Poles."

A woman from San Francisco who has worked with Soviet Jews "felt a disturbing familiarity in the accounts which you recorded and the intricate apologetics I've heard from Soviet Jews about anti-Semitism. It was hard to know what to say to these people when I would hear the most blatantly anti-Semitic 'analyses' of history being solemnly explained to me. . . . While deploring it, Americans can at least understand the process of government-sanctioned anti-Semitism in Eastern Europe. But it is much more difficult to comprehend the degree to which these racist attitudes have become woven into the fabric of those societies." This reader questioned in particular "the (supposed) facts about the percentage of Jews in the Polish Communist party. I've found that those stories turn out to be the Eastern European equivalent of the 'Jews control the U.S. media and all U.S. corporations' type of misinformation with which we've all become too familiar."

On the other hand, a Brooklyn Heights Jewish emigré from Poland wrote to disassociate himself from the comments of the Los Angeles emigré quoted in my article who felt that the calamities currently visiting Poland couldn't have happened to a more deserving people: "I find this statement reprehensible and difficult to understand and accept as I too experienced hunger in Poland during the war and I am far from indifferent but rather very compassionate and troubled by the knowledge that in the country, in the city, in the house where I and my forefathers lived, there are children who are hungry . . . . Some of my friends who have the same background and have had the same experience as Jews in Poland feel exactly as I do and do not feel the vindictiveness expressed by our counterpart in Los Angeles."

3. This brief, curious war between the Soviets and the Poles in 1920 commands an extraordinarily important place in the Polish imagination. The various campaigns and countercampaigns of 1920 took place against a double backdrop. To begin with, there was the almost simultaneous upsurge of Bolshevism in both Russia and Germany at the conclusion of the war. (By some accounts, the Soviet army was in part attempting to cross Poland in order to lend assistance to the besieged Communist communes in postwar Prussia and Bavaria.) Secondly, these battles took place during the period of the Versailles Conference, when the newly sovereign state of Poland was attempting to lay claim to the widest possible territory—specifically, to reestablish its borders as they existed before the first of the partitions that completely

obliterated Poland in 1772. The August battle on the outskirts of
Warsaw had actually been preceded, four months earlier, by a
battle just outside Kiev, in the Ukraine. Indeed, it was only
because the Polish army's Ukraine offensive had become so ridiculously overextended during the spring that the Soviet counter-
offensive was in turn able to drive the Poles all the way back to
Warsaw during the summer. In the Treaty of Riga (1921), Poland managed to secure most of its claims on Soviet territory—an
outcome that the Kremlin would not forget and that would contribute to Soviet diplomacy twenty years later (the Nazi-Soviet
Nonaggression Pact).

It turns out that the unknown soldier in the Tomb of the
Unknown Soldier in Warsaw died not in one of the world wars,
but rather in the Polish-Soviet War of 1920. The Poles have long
relished the spectacle of Soviet and Polish Communist Party officials delivering their ritual wreaths to the monument at official
functions several times each year.

4. Following *Proba Mikrofonu,* Lozinski went on to concoct a
remarkable feature film—part documentary and part fiction—
entitled *Jak Zyc (How to Live).* Shot before August, 1980, it, like
the earlier film, was only released after that summer. The film's
poster, suddenly visible all over Warsaw this spring, gives a clue
as to why release was delayed. It shows a large stone bust with a
cravat dangling from the neck and instead of a face, a simple
word engraved into the stonebulb: "TAK" ("Yes").

Jak Zyc documents an astonishing few weeks at a summer camp
for young Communist families. The camp—a reward for "good
behavior"—was used until recently as an incentive to keep young
Party bureaucrats in line, and invariably turned into a festival
for sycophants. Although Lozinski inserts a few actors of his own
into the camp, most of the action in the film (specifically the
Orwellian competition to determine "the best young Communist
family," in which everyone was graded daily on a variety of nu-
merical indices and children were encouraged to rat on parents,
and families to undermine one another's orthodoxy) was actually
happening at the camp anyway.

In a recent interview, Lozinski noted that repression during the
Gierek era may have been just as virulent as before, although it
wore a different face: "Certainly during the seventies there were
no mass arrests or (after 1970) bloody solutions. But please note

that the mechanism was different. The dominant system of 'social education' was a system of rewards and privileges instead of a system of punishment." Later on in the interview, when asked how the people at the camp reacted to the presence of his cameras, Lozinski replied, "They were convinced that, since we were from Warsaw, we were something like another TV crew. Indeed, the staff people at the camp (the ones who were scoring the competition) may have performed their functions even more assiduously than usual, perhaps expecting that, in line with the reward system, the film would presently be seen by their own superiors."

5. It is an occasion for sad reflection to gauge the very different qualities of this interpenetration in Poland and the United States today. In Poland, cinema and politics reflect and confirm each other's vitality and significance; in America, our actor-president merely highlights the emptiness of our image-addled political process.

6. The anchor, a longtime token of Polish-Catholic nationalism, has had a rich history in Gdansk. After 1970, several of the graves in the Gdansk cemeteries, otherwise unmarked, consisted of simple white crosses bearing small crucified Christ figures from the feet of which (an inverse image) hung modest anchors. These mark the graves of the noncorpses from the December massacre.

7. This distinction between "political" and "social" concerns predates the current Polish situation. Indeed, across much of the early parts of his classic chronicle of the 1917 Russian Revolution, *Ten Days That Shook the World,* John Reed goes to great lengths to portray the different conceptions of revolution championed by the Mensheviks, on the one hand, and the Bolsheviks, on the other. Whereas the Mensheviks, according to Reed, were satisfied to limit their revolution to the "political" sphere, the Bolsheviks insisted on carrying it into the "social" realm as well. "Having at one bound leaped from the Middle Ages into the twentieth century," Reed concludes, "Russia showed the startled world two systems of revolution—the political and the social—in mortal combat." (Penguin edition, 1977, p. 36). Of course, its Bolshevik lineage renders Solidarity's position all the more interesting.

8. Contemporary economic policy in the United States affords an interesting contrast to this Polish approach. Under Reagan's

tax plan, the recent cuts have been made on a same-percentage-for-everyone basis, with the result that rich people are getting breaks amounting to thousands of dollars each, while poor people get nothing at all. The contrast could hardly be more galling.

9. Daniel Singer's book includes an appendix in which he details the extraordinary evolution of the consciousness of the Polish working class during the summer of 1980. "Although I was one of the few Western writers to go quite as far out on a limb as I did," Singer told me during a conversation in his Paris home, "I must say I did not anticipate the movement's being as mature or as adult as it's been. Much of that maturation however, occurred during August itself and perhaps couldn't have been anticipated. This is something which Western theorists have tended to downplay: the extraordinary capacity for people's maturing under pressure. I have spoken with several of the Polish intellectual 'experts' who were called to Gdansk by the workers about a week after the strike began, and they all tell the same story. Here they were, fresh from Warsaw, and their first bit of expert insight was that there was no possibility of obtaining an independent free trade union, so that they were coming in with all sorts of compromise proposals. And instead they were immediately told by everybody, from the first worker they met up to the presidium of the strike committee, that on that issue there could be no budging. Anything else was negotiable, but not that. Now, the idea of an independent trade union was something that, ten days before, maybe twenty people throughout the labor force of the Gdansk region had even thought of. I mean, implicitly perhaps, many thousands favored the idea, but they didn't even know it. And in ten short days, this demand for free and independent trade unions was to become the central expression of the will of the whole of the working class of the maritime region, and within a few more days, of the entire country. It's quite amazing."

10. "The only democratic counterforce to vanguard (Leninist) politics or to corporate politics," Lawrence Goodwyn, the historian of American populism, wrote in a recent article in the new quarterly *Democracy* "is a politically democratic presence in society—that is, some kind of empowered and democratic polity. Such an organized democratic presence is quite literally the most fundamental threat conceivable to the continuing dominance of corporate and vanguard elites. The historical evidence is over-

whelming that both will, when confronted with even the beginnings of an autonomous democratic presence, move promptly to destroy it, divert it, buy it, or try in any way to gain effective control over it."

Goodwyn's formulation helps explain a certain wary reserve which was evident among many American corporatists and bankers as they observed the bourgeoning of Solidarity. Secretary of State Alexander Haig and some of the other alarmists in the new Reagan Administration had some more immediate tactical considerations in mind as well during those days when they seemed almost to be wishing for a Soviet invasion. For starters, the Soviet Union's ongoing restraint in the Polish situation during the spring and summer of 1981 was running absolutely counter to everything the hard-line anti-Soviet ideologues in the new Reagan State Department would have had Americans believe about Soviet intentions and capabilities. Far from appearing power glutted and ambition crazed, the Kremlin leadership was appearing either too weak or too circumspect to take decisive action in its own interests on its very borders. Indeed, the Soviet Union seemed, if anything, a "pitiful giant"—hardly, at any rate, the kind of fearsome opponent which might justify "massive defense spending increases" on the American side.

Were the Soviet Union to have invaded Poland, on the other hand, hard-liners in the Reagan Administration could have anticipated two very handsome side-benefits. First of all, the Soviet Union's macrostrategic situation would in reality have been decisively weakened. Its armed forces would suddenly have found themselves bogged down on two fronts—both in Afghanistan and Poland—neither with any hope of short-term resolution. At the same time, the Soviet Union's diplomatic standing would have suffered an overwhelming firestorm, particularly in Western Europe, where the longing for détente had failed to subside nearly as quickly as it had in the United States. Thus, the Soviet Union after a Polish invasion would in reality have constituted a substantially weaker opponent and yet—and here was the second side-benefit—it would have appeared to be a stronger, more threatening one. Imagine the ease with which the American military lobby could have subdued the growing disarmament movement in Europe were the Soviet Union merely to have cooperated by launching a few hundred thousand troops across its western borders.

Some commentators have noted that the Haig State Department's fixation on this question of Soviet intervention inadvertently (or, insist some cynics, intentionally) gave Polish authorities the impression that Washington would not object to an exclusively Polish military solution to the deteriorating political situation.

11. For a more complete discussion of the role of posters and graphic imagery in the achievement of Solidarity, see my article "Solidarnosc," in the February 1982 issue of *Artforum.*

12. The actual figure posted at banks and hotels early in September is 34.22 zlotys to the dollar. Point twenty-two. Since this rate bears no relationship whatsoever to the actual value of the currency, and since American banks and institutions aren't accepting zlotys in payment for their dollar debts in any case, it remains one of the enduring mysteries of travel in Poland just how the authorities come up with their official rates. Why point twenty-two? Why not point twenty-seven or point sixty-one? Somebody no doubt gets paid good money (probably dollars) to think these figures up and then monkey with them from week to week.

13. One afternoon in Warsaw I was speaking with a woman graduate student at the University. I asked her what kinds of political concerns she'd had before 1980. "Mainly involving feminist issues," she replied. "But since last August, I think a lot of us have set some of those concerns aside for the time being. They're important, but at the moment there are some things that are more important—the salvaging of the entire nation, for example—and the solidarity of the movement is the most important of all."

14. There were even some people I talked with who, in the tradition of Polish Romantic messianism, believed that if the Russians invaded, the Poles would *win!* The scenario I was frequently offered conjured up a Russian army bogged down in Poland for months, maybe years, of bloody guerrilla fighting, while one by one the other Warsaw Pact countries—whose armies, incidentally, would likewise be detained on Polish soil—would become engulfed in working class rebellions of their own, rebellions that would eventually spread into the Soviet Union itself, leading to the collapse of the Kremlin regime. Q.E.D.

15. During the final days of the congress, KOR itself disbanded, and its forty activists simply became members of the union their courageous stand had originally helped to found. Many observers interpreted the group's dissolution as an attempt to calm Soviet hysteria: if so, the attempt failed. KOR had for some time served as a lightning rod, protecting Solidarity itself, in some perverse way, from the full brunt of Soviet attacks; now the Soviet media charged that the union was being infiltrated by the most anti-socialist elements in Polish society.

This last charge was answered quite eloquently by Edward Lipinski, the ninety-three-year-old economist who has served as a spiritual father to the Polish dissident movement for some time (indeed, KOR was founded in 1976 in his apartment). Speaking from the podium of the congress, the frail man read the delegates KOR's "last will and testament" with a booming voice and then concluded, "I consider myself a socialist. I have been a socialist since 1906. Socialism was to be the solving of the problems of the working class, the liberation of the working class, the creation of conditions in which every man could become fully developed. But the socialism that was created here was a socialism of mis-management and inefficiency that brought about economic ca-tastrophe unequalled in two hundred years. It is a socialism of prisons, censorship, and police. This socialism has been destroy-ing us for thirty-odd years as it has been destroying others. It is this socialism that is antisocialist and antirevolutionary."